INTO THE
HINTERLAND

TINA SHAW

Published by Pearson Education Limited, Edinburgh Gate, Harlow, Essex, CM20 2JE.

www.pearsonschools.co.uk

First published by Pearson New Zealand
a division of Pearson New Zealand Ltd
67 Apollo Drive, Rosedale, North Shore 0632, New Zealand
Associated companies throughout the world

Text © Pearson Education New Zealand 2007
Original edition edited by Lucy Armour
Original edition designed by Suzanne Wesley
This edition designed by Sara Rafferty

The right of Tina Shaw to be identified as author of this work has been asserted by her in accordance with the Copyright, Designs and Patents Act 1988.

First published 2007
This edition published 2013

17 16 15 14 13
10 9 8 7 6 5 4 3 2 1

British Library Cataloguing in Publication Data
A catalogue record for this book is available from the British Library

ISBN 978 0 435 14435 7

Printed in Malaysia (CTP-VP)

Acknowledgements
We would like to thank Bangor Central Integrated Primary School, Northern Ireland; Bishop Henderson Church of England Primary School, Somerset; Bletchingdon Parochial Church of England Primary School, Oxfordshire; Brookside Community Primary School, Somerset; Bude Park Primary School, Hull; Cheddington Combined School, Buckinghamshire; Dair House Independent School, Buckinghamshire; Glebe Infant School, Gloucestershire; Henley Green Primary School, Coventry; Lovelace Primary School, Surrey; Our Lady of Peace Junior School, Slough; Tackley Church of England Primary School, Oxfordshire; and Twyford Church of England School, Buckinghamshire for their invaluable help in the development and trialling of the Bug Club resources.

Every effort has been made to contact copyright holders of material reproduced in this book. Any omissions will be rectified in subsequent printings if notice is given to the publishers.

A division of Pearson New Zealand Ltd

Contents

BASSORAH
TO THE LAKE
THE MILL
THE KEEP
VANCY'S ROCK
THE HINTERLAND
TEM'S DEVICE
TEM'S DWELLING
FORTRESS

Prologue

Many years ago ...

The man carried the baby out into the desert. He held the swaddled bundle loosely in one arm, like a sack of gravel. When he reached the boulder, he paused, squinting into the distance. Perhaps he was expecting to see something. But there was only the flat, rocky wilderness that was the Hinterland. It went on for miles and miles, and there wasn't another person in sight.

The man put the baby on the rock.

The sun was just coming up. Soon, it would be very hot. It was the height of the dry season. Not even a fully-grown man would find it easy to sit out here all day in the heat, with no water — let alone a baby. A baby would probably last only a few hours. If the sun didn't do its work, the hyenas would. What might this baby have become if it weren't left in the desert? Nobody would know now.

The baby lay quietly on top of the boulder. She was very young, yet she made no sound or whimper. Her steely grey eyes stared at the looming figure of the man. Perhaps the baby saw only a large, dark shape but, to the man's mind, her eyes seemed to judge him.

"It might not be your fault," growled the man, as if answering a question, "but this is what happens."

As the sun came up over the horizon, casting its first hot rays across the land, the man turned on his heel and walked back towards a large, stone-walled building at the base of the mountains.

In the west, there was a movement, a shimmer of silver heading towards the boulder. The shimmer took on the shape of a dog. A large, silvery dog.

The dog stopped at the boulder and bent over the baby. With eyes wide, the child opened her mouth, as if to squawk. The dog slipped a small stone into the baby's mouth.

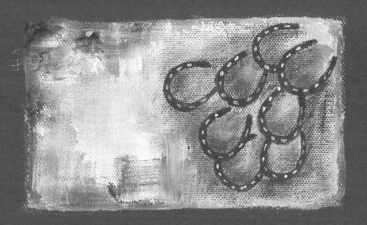

I

"Vancy, are you coming to my party tonight?"

Vancy looked up from the gate of the pony enclosure, which she was about to unlatch. Kerei was blinking and grinning at her like a startled gerbil. Why did she have to look after him? He might be turning fifteen and having a "coming-of-age" party, she thought, silently snorting at the idea, but he was pathetic. If he wasn't fooling around with that silly friend of his, he was quivering in his boots.

"Come on, Van, what d'you say? Everybody's going to be there."

The girl gave a half-hearted shrug. Everybody from the community might be at Kerei's house tonight, but she wouldn't be. Stupid celebrations. What was the big deal in turning fifteen anyway? Why couldn't they all just shut up about it and leave her alone? She knocked the bucket of greens against the fence to let the ponies know she was coming.

Kerei was jiggling up and down with barely contained excitement. "I can't wait. It's going to be brilliant."

"Yeah," muttered Vancy, "but right now we have to catch one of the ponies for the Mill, remember?"

"Oh, sure, sure," he said quickly.

Each morning one of the stocky ponies had to be caught and placed in the mill shaft, where it would spend the next three hours pushing the stones that ground the corn or barley or wheat into flour. After three hours it would be replaced with another pony. Somebody had to catch the ponies. That was Vancy's job. Nobody else wanted to do it. But one day, she thought, Kerei could do it by himself. Especially if she wasn't here to do it for him.

Vancy unlatched the gate and entered the pony enclosure. She knew Kerei was afraid of the ponies, but she didn't care. Serve him right if he got bitten. It might stop him going on about his stupid party.

Bucket in hand, she walked towards the dark stalls where the ponies sheltered. None of them was out yet, but Vancy knew they would be listening, heads lowered. They would have heard the gate being unlatched. Now they waited, eyes gleaming in the dark.

Vancy stopped and gave a low whistle.

"What're you doing?" Kerei croaked behind her.

She was supposed to be training him, but that didn't mean she had to *tell* him anything. Let him learn the hard way, she thought. Taking a step forward, she made a single click with her tongue. A small grey pony, with hair down to its withers, rushed out from the stalls.

Kerei gasped and jumped backwards, banging against the enclosure wall. Two more ponies raced out of the stalls. They pulled to a stop in front of Vancy, nudging and whinnying. "Look at that," she said. "Nothing to worry about. They're just like puppies. Totally harmless."

"Yeah," muttered Kerei, as if he'd like to melt into the wall. "As long as you don't get too close to them."

Vancy loved being with the ponies. It was the one place in Bassorah where she felt truly at home. She understood the ponies. And they accepted her. They would let her scratch them behind the ears and slip on the halter. Other people found them too difficult, even her foster father Erik, who ran the Mill. If she carried out the plan she had in her mind, she would miss the ponies.

Vancy glanced back at Kerei. "You can feed them now," she said. It was a command rather than a suggestion.

The boy edged towards her, trying to keep away from the back ends of the ponies. Vancy held the bucket out to him. The ponies strained their snouts up to bunt the bottom of the bucket, wanting their treat.

"I don't know why you're so scared of them," she teased.

"Well," said Kerei, taking the bucket, "there're those horrible teeth for a start."

He was probably thinking of Mag – one of the ponies had bitten her arm, leaving a nasty bruise. But if the ponies took against certain people, you couldn't really blame them. You just had to know how to handle them.

"And then there's the nasty little hooves."

"At least you don't have the job of trimming

their hooves," mused Vancy. "Though maybe I'll show you that next… "

Kerei wrinkled his nose, but made no reply.

Vancy stood back and watched, arms crossed over her chest, as Kerei fed leaves from the bucket to the hungry ponies. He was doing it all wrong. Half the leaves were dropping on the ground and getting crushed beneath the ponies' hooves. They wouldn't like that. And Kerei was gibbering to himself. They wouldn't like that either. The ponies were highly-strung and had to be treated with care. They could smell fear, which would only make things worse for Kerei. Why had Kerei, of all people, been assigned to the Mill? He was hopeless.

Another two latecomers came galloping around the bend and came to a halt at the last minute, their tiny hooves throwing up dust. They had seen the bucket and knew their treat was in it. Beady eyes were fixed on Kerei. He held the bucket high and, like a magician, pulled out handfuls of leaves. The ponies, in their eagerness, jostled around him. Seeing that he was being pushed back towards the stone wall of the enclosure, Vancy moved out of the way.

Noses and mouths nudged at the boy's hand, clamping over leaves that he couldn't get out fast enough. No sooner was one bunch grabbed and greedily munched by yellow teeth, than other mouths were butting him for more.

"Here you are," Kerei gasped. "Take it easy … there's enough for all of you."

But there wasn't. Kerei, his eyes on the ponies, felt around inside the bucket, only to find there were no leaves left. But the ponies were still hungry. They shoved him, mouths dripping with green saliva. His back was now against the wall.

Kerei turned the empty bucket towards them. "Look – no more."

One pony put his snout inside the bucket, making a grunting noise like a pig.

"All gone," said Kerei in a high-pitched voice.

"If I were you," said Vancy, leaning against the wall, "I'd get out of here pretty fast."

Kerei looked at the milling crush of ponies. There was an evil look in their eyes now, as if they planned to rip him to shreds the way they had devoured the leaves. Then, with a shout, he leapt into the air.

"Ow! I've been bitten!" he yelped, and raced for the gate. The mob of ponies raced after him, heads extended and lips drawn back, their tiny hooves pounding like hail on a tin roof.

Kerei vaulted the low gate. He stumbled, gasping for breath, then looked back. Six pairs of eyes were glaring at him.

Vancy was laughing.

"You could've *done* something," he cried. "They might've killed me!"

Now he really did sound like a snivelling little kid. Coming of age, huh! "Killed you?" Vancy put her hands out to the ponies, which were now drifting back to surround her. She gave a soft laugh. "I don't think so."

Vancy sat in the darkest corner of the room, hugging her knees. With glittering eyes, she watched the festivities. She had intended to disappear to her favourite spot – the high rock that overlooked the Hinterland – but Lisbet had caught her sneaking out the back door.

"Where are you going, young lady?"

Vancy had tried to shrug off her foster mother's

hand, but Lisbet had a firm grasp on her shoulder.

"I hope you weren't planning to hide away," said Lisbet sternly. "It's your friend's special day, and you must be here, too."

"He's not my friend," Vancy muttered from between clenched teeth.

"Now, now," sighed Lisbet, pushing the girl back into the house. "No jealousy, please."

"But it's not fair," Vancy had cried, hearing the whine in her voice.

Her foster mother's lined face softened. Still holding her by the shoulder, Lisbet turned Vancy around so she could look into her daughter's eyes. "You know, it's just the way it is," she said gently.

Tears had stung Vancy's eyes then. "I *don't* know," she said petulantly, sounding as childish as Kerei. "I'll be fifteen soon and I ought to have a party, too. It's not fair!"

Lisbet sighed and dropped her eyes. "I know, Vancy. But it's just the way it is. This isn't about you."

"Of course it's about me," Vancy had shouted, pulling away from Lisbet. "I'm not one of you," she spat, "and I never will be!"

Tears had run down her cheeks. They didn't care. None of them did. Lisbet and Erik could've had a party for her, too, only they wouldn't. They were too old to go against the Council. But they *could* have.

Vancy had flung herself down in a corner and stared furiously at the ceiling. Stupid party. There was no difference between being fourteen and fifteen anyway. Nothing changed just because you had a stupid party.

Almost the entire community was packed into Kerei's house. Huddled in her corner, Vancy was forced to see what she herself would never get. No party for her – she was the outsider and always would be.

She had seen people coming and going all day, bringing food and gifts. The tables were laden. The guests were singing and linking arms to dance their funny dance. Vancy still found the dancing odd, even though she had grown up in Bassorah. It was as if the foreign part of her, deep down, was being critical.

Vancy's foster parents, Erik and Lisbet, were

sitting on chairs against the wall. They sat stiffly, faces lit by the lantern light, hands linked across their laps, while the others danced and sang. Vancy thought they looked lonely, separate. Why couldn't they just get up and dance like the others?

Her real parents would be dancing.

But, of course, Erik and Lisbet were old. They would've been old when they took her in as a baby; everybody else already had children. Vancy wondered what was going through their minds. They were probably thinking about how she, Vancy, wouldn't ever get a party like this, she thought bitterly.

Erik had practically said as much the other day when Vancy had asked if she, too, would get a party when she turned fifteen. Her foster father had turned away, a hand to his chin. He hadn't needed to say anything. She *knew*. How could she even expect it? After all, she wasn't one of them. Not truly, not blood – whatever *that* meant. It was stupid, a stupid rule made up about a hundred years ago by the Council. It meant nothing!

A commotion at the front door made her look up. Several men came bustling in, bearing Kerei on their shoulders. They were all laughing, red-faced and happy. True, it was a holiday, but the apple cider would've helped as well. Ah yes, the ritual! The fifteen-year-old was carried over the threshold of his parents' house to mark the end of childhood. His next step across the threshold, they said, would be as a man. Huh, thought Vancy, gutless Kerei wasn't going to grow up overnight!

She watched as the men dumped Kerei in the middle of the room. There was much clapping and cheering. Kerei's mother, over in the corner, was dabbing at her eyes with a corner of her apron. At least he had a real mother. Vancy didn't know where *her* real mother was – she didn't even know her name.

She looked at her fingers, rough and unlovely, with dirt under the nails. She linked them together over her knees. A tumult of feelings raced through her. Mostly, there was envy. Why Kerei and not her? She had been part of this community since she was a baby. Why not *her* as well?

Kerei had got to his feet now, and the men were linking arms for another one of their stupid dances. The guitarist in the corner was playing so hard his face gleamed with sweat. Everybody was so happy – it made her sick. Soon they would bring out the huge platters of fruits and sweets. She'd vomit if she saw any more food.

This time, nobody noticed as Vancy crept along the wall and out the front door.

The house was silent and dark. Vancy hurried to her room and dug out a woven bag from under her bed. Into this bag she stuffed some clothes, her knife, a hat and a coat. In the kitchen, she took almond patties from the safe and wrapped them in heavy waxed paper, quickly tying the package with brown string. And water: she'd need that where she was going. Grabbing a spare skin from the back of the kitchen door, she filled it with water from the jug. She just hoped it would be enough.

With a final backward glance, she stepped outside and shut the door behind her. Hurrying up the street, she thought how nobody would miss her until the next day. The party would go on for hours yet, even though Lisbet and Erik would probably get tired and leave early. But, when Lisbet looked into her room, the pillows beneath the covers would look like Vancy, fast asleep.

Maybe she should leave a note? Vancy paused, looking back down the empty cobbled street. Too late, she decided, with a tug of regret. She wanted to get a head start, before a Patrol was sent out to find her. There wasn't even time to say goodbye to her ponies.

Vancy hurried on. At the top of the rise, she turned sharply left and entered the trees. There was no path here. They weren't supposed to explore this side of the ridge. But Vancy knew the way well enough, even in the dark. A short way in, she came to the goat track that led to her favourite rock – a small boulder that overlooked the vast Hinterland. It was a place to watch the sun set, and to think.

But tonight, Vancy wasn't going to her rock. She was going to a special place she had discovered quite by accident. She was the only one who knew about this place. Her own little secret, it was a narrow, cave-like tunnel that led out into the Hinterland, barely wide enough for a girl to wriggle through. But it was the only way out of Bassorah aside from the Pass, which was always guarded. And, unlike the Pass, there was nobody guarding this place.

Vancy got down on her knees and shoved the bag ahead of her. Carefully, she crawled into the tunnel. During the day, there was enough light to see where you were going, but at night it was bitter black. Vancy didn't let the darkness put her off. She had been through here enough times to know what to expect. Many times she had sneaked outside Bassorah, to be by herself. She liked the Hinterland – it was quiet and vast. Out there, the sky was like a great big bowl. It was so different from Bassorah, where all you ever saw were trees or crowded stone buildings. People talked about Herit's Fortress, somewhere out in the Hinterland, but Bassorah, in its own way, was also a fortress. In the Hinterland, there was so much space you felt like an eagle.

Finally, Vancy was out. She hauled herself upright and looked around, surveying the empty moonlit plain before her. She hadn't been out here at night before. The air smelt clean and earthy. She raised her chin, feeling deeply excited. With one last backward glance at the rock walls that enclosed Bassorah, she turned and headed west.

II

Kerei returned home very pleased with himself. Vancy hadn't been at the Mill that morning. She was so … well, difficult. Always waiting for him to trip up, to make a fool of himself, so she could have a laugh at his expense. Understandably, it made him nervous. Which is why he probably hadn't been much good with those ponies. Horrible, smelly things. Besides, without Vancy around, the ponies seemed easier to deal with. They knew where their next meal was coming from, and this morning it had been from Kerei.

Little stinkers. He hated working with the ponies. Most of the boys wanted to be assigned to the Keep and stay up with the Night Watch. But no, his father said he was too young for that.

He'd have to wait, even though he'd reached the age of maturity. He would have to stick it out at the Mill for a few months, and then he could start pestering his father about another job.

In the meantime, he was hungry. He intended to have a snack, then maybe a swim up at the lake.

"Hello?" he called.

The main room was empty. The wall mats were rolled up to allow the breeze to filter through the house from the courtyard. Kerei poked his head through the door of his parents' room. Also empty. He shrugged. His father was probably out working with the others in the fields, planting or something. Kerei went back to the kitchen and checked out the hanging safe, looking for food. There was a plate of tapioca honey cakes. He devoured several before he heard a noise, and his father stepped into the house from the courtyard.

Kerei's father was a large man with wiry hair. His loose shirt was grimy and there was a smear of earth on his cheek. "I'd swear you've got hollow legs," he said to Kerei.

"Is there any more food?" asked the boy. "I'm starving."

His father chuckled and walked over to the low table in the middle of the room. He opened one of the drawers. "Here, I was saving them for myself, but it looks as if you need them more than me," he said, handing Kerei a box of almond patties. Thick, meaty and filling, they were just what Kerei needed to fill the last gaps. His father eyed him with interest. "So, how was it today?"

"All right," mumbled Kerei through a mouthful of patty.

They sat on the soft couches around the table. Kerei sprawled, stretching out his long legs.

"And Vancy?" his father asked.

Kerei shrugged. "I dunno. She wasn't there."

"Is she sick?"

"How should I know?" Kerei gave a snort. He stuffed the rest of the almond patty into his mouth and leaned over, chewing, to unlace his boots. "She's a *mumble mumble mumble*," he said to his feet.

"Excuse me, a what?" His father was grinning.

Kerei, his mouth no longer full, politely clarified: "She's one really tough girl." He sat up, slinging an arm along the back of the couch. "But I just wish she'd help me out a bit more," he continued. "She's supposed to be training me. But she doesn't tell me anything. And, when I get something wrong, she just laughs at me. I don't get it."

"She certainly is a strange one," his father said thoughtfully.

"Tell me again how they found her."

His father studied the whitewashed wall. Kerei could tell that it wasn't the flaking plaster he was looking at, but a scene from another time. "It was a funny day. Your mother was unwell, and I had stayed back from the fields to be with her, so I didn't see exactly how it happened. But a baby was left at the edge of the fields by a large dog. A silver dog. Nobody even knew how it had got in – or where it had come from."

Kerei snorted impatiently. "How could a dog carry a baby?"

His father shrugged. "The baby was wrapped in something. Perhaps the dog had carried it that way."

"I'm surprised it didn't just eat her."

"Well, obviously it didn't."

"So what else?" Kerei asked. "That's the *official* story. But I know there's more to it than that. And what about this mysterious dog?"

His father glanced up. "I don't know any more than you do, son. It was a big silver dog, which we all supposed had come out of the Hinterland. I mean, where else would it have come from? How it got up to the fields, though, is a different story. Nobody saw it at the Pass. The dog came like a ghost, is all I know, and left the same way."

"So," drawled Kerei, voicing a private thought, "Vancy probably came from the Hinterland."

"It does seem likely," said his father. "There's nowhere else she – or the dog – *could* have come from."

"From Herit's Fortress?" Kerei asked eagerly.

His father gave an embarrassed cough. "For all we know, there may be other people living out there. Groups of nomads, perhaps."

Kerei pondered this. It didn't seem likely.

He looked out at the leafy apple tree in the courtyard, growing up between the stone flags. A warm breeze shifted through the room.

Nobody came from the Hinterland. It was a place dominated by their enemy. The question was – and always had been – was Vancy one of the enemy as well? The village had brought her up like one of their own – had even given her a name – but there was always this unspoken doubt. What if one day the enemy wanted her back? Babies didn't just get taken away by silver dogs without people worrying about where they'd gone. How he would love to see one of those famous silver dogs. People said that the mangy dogs in their own village had descended from silver dogs, though you wouldn't think it to look at them.

"Well," said Kerei, giving a terrific yawn, "that's all very interesting. But I wish I had somebody else training me."

Kerei's father gave him a playful cuff on his way out. "Take it easy, son."

"Hey, wait," cried Kerei, leaning over the couch just as his father was about to step out into the courtyard. "Isn't Mother back yet?"

His father rubbed a hand across his eyes. Both father and son worried when Kerei's mother was away. "Your mother's still out with the Patrol," he said abruptly, before disappearing altogether.

Kerei walked up the street and past the stone houses, a towel slung over his shoulder. The place was deserted. Nearly all of the community were up at the fields during the day. There was a caramel dog dozing in a patch of sunlight. It awoke as Kerei walked past and started to follow him up the hill. Kerei heard the pattering of paws behind him and stopped. The dog, he noticed, had a dirty white patch around one eye. Descended from silver dogs, huh! Descended, more like it, from the hyenas that occasionally tried to creep in through the Pass, only to feel the jab of an arrow or spear.

Kerei bent down and gripped the dog's head, eyeballing the animal. "What d'you know about silver dogs, eh?" he asked.

The dog cocked its head, as if considering the question.

Kerei dropped his voice to a whisper. "Are you a silver dog in disguise?" he asked. "Blink once for yes, twice for no." The dog glanced to one side, as if wondering how to get away from this strange human.

"Hey, you!" called a voice behind Kerei. "What are you doing with that poor mutt?"

Kerei released the dog. "It's none of your business if I want to have a serious discussion with a dog," he retorted.

The other boy laughed and hooked his arm around Kerei's neck, giving him a playful squeeze. "I don't know about that," he said. "That dog might be a spy, and you might've been telling him important information." The boy's arm tightened against Kerei's windpipe.

Kerei shook him off. "What are you doing out here anyway, turnip-head? Aren't you supposed to be in the fields with the others?"

Squirt rolled his eyes. "I'm sick of sticking beans in the dirt and pulling out weeds from between carrots." The two boys started to walk side by side up the hill. "And don't call me turnip-head. My head is much more attractive than a turnip!"

"All right then, how about radish-brain?"

"You're the one with the radish brain."

Kerei poked his friend in the ribs. "Maybe you are jealous that I'm on the Mill now and you're still sticking beans in dirt."

"Yeah, as if." Squirt shrugged. "I'd much rather be on the Keep."

"Me, too," agreed Kerei, though secretly he thought it might be a bit scary up there at night.

They reached the top of the rise. A path on the right went through trees, over the ridge and on to the lake. Another path forked away down the other side, towards the fields.

"Still, you're the lucky one," muttered Squirt. "I'm fed up with planting and harvesting and digging and all that boring stuff!"

Kerei glanced sideways at his friend. He hadn't heard Squirt talk like that before. Everybody was used to the field work and all the other duties that came with living in a small, sheltered community. You hardly ever heard anybody complain. It was something they had grown up with, from when they were babies. It was just what they did.

Squirt grabbed Kerei's arm and pulled him off the path and under a tree, so that the branches shielded them from anyone who might walk past.

"I want to *do* something. I want an adventure," he said in a low voice. "I'm sick of planting and harvesting. It's so boring here. I want to *live*!" His breath was hot and peanutty against Kerei's neck. "Don't you ever wonder what's out there?"

Kerei tried to shake off Squirt's grip, but his

friend held on fast. Of course he had wondered what was out there from time to time. But, mostly, he didn't want to worry about it too much. He left that to other people, people like his mother.

"Look," said Squirt, "we're not kids any more. You're on the Mill now. At least you've got some responsibility." That was sort of true, thought Kerei. "Well, I want to do something, too," Squirt continued fiercely. "I want to go out into the Hinterland!"

The Hinterland again – where his mother was patrolling. Kerei pulled free of Squirt's grip. His friend's eyes were burning and he had a feverish, pale look about his mouth.

"You're crazy," said Kerei soberly, drawing himself up a little. The last few days working at the Mill, as well as his coming-of-age party, had already wrought some subtle changes in Kerei. He was no longer the kid who Squirt used to dunk in the lake. "People don't go out there until they're at least twenty. And, besides, they're picked to go out there. You can't just decide to go out." Then he added hotly, stabbing home his point, "Anyway, you're too young."

There were white marks on Kerei's arm

where his friend's fingers had gripped him. Squirt blinked at him, then dropped back a step to stare beyond Kerei's shoulder, into the light bush. "What's too young?" he asked intently, giving Kerei's shoulder a light punch. "Eh?"

Then he was gone, running back down the hill. The caramel dog, now sitting in the shade, looked enquiringly at Kerei, as if to ask what that had been about. Kerei shook his head and took himself along the path to the lake.

That night, thunder crackled in the air. By the time Kerei's mother returned from a week's duty with the Patrol, it was late. Kerei was woken by the sound of voices coming from the main room. He wandered into the dark hallway to see what was happening and heard his mother say: "I don't know how long we can hold them back." She almost sounded ill with seriousness. Rubbing his eyes, Kerei leaned against the wall to listen.

"But isn't it always just like this?" It was his father's voice, low and deep.

"This is different," murmured his mother. "There are more groups of them out there. Some kind of activity. I think something might be about to happen."

Kerei rested his bare shoulder against the cool stone of the wall. He hoped that wasn't going to be all they said. A shiver ran down his spine.

It was his father who spoke next, even more quietly. "We have thought that before."

"Yes," said his mother slowly, "but I have a bad feeling this time."

"Then we need to be prepared," sighed his father.

"Yes, I know," she said. "And not just the Patrols. We will *all* need to be prepared."

There was the sound of movement, as if one of them had got up. Feeling spooked, Kerei padded silently back to his room. He wondered what all the fuss was about. Then he thought about Squirt wanting to go off into the Hinterland. Yeah, maybe Squirt should talk to Kerei's mother. She'd put him straight on that score. It was dangerous out there – everybody knew that. They were all better off here, behind the high rocky walls of Bassorah. Nice and safe.

III

First night out in the Hinterland, and it was scary. Vancy had thought there would be birds out here, and the friendly rustle of small night creatures. Those things would've made her feel better. But, as she lay down in a little hollow, she heard nothing. It was an eerie kind of silence, broken only by the breeze running through the clumps of grass. It made a sad sound: low and sighing.

Vancy curled up as best she could in the hollow. The ground was hard. Something was prickly under her cheek and she shifted the arm of her coat so she was more comfortable. The Hinterland was so vast – she hadn't realised that until tonight, when she had walked and walked towards the western star, and still there was nothing except the dim expanse of plain ahead of her.

She had never felt so alone.

Turning on to her back, Vancy looked up at the enormous dish of stars and black sky. She could be the only living thing out here on the plains. That was better than some of the stories she had heard, though. Such as the one about packs of hyenas. But they hunted during the day, didn't they? Nervously, Vancy pulled the knife from her bag and laid it within easy reach. She hadn't thought much about hyenas before. She'd been too busy thinking about how to find her real parents.

Vancy's mind began to drift. What if there was nothing out here except Herit's Fortress? She looked at the cold stars, feeling even smaller. She had always imagined other communities like Bassorah, or small villages in the mountains. Bassorah itself was part of the mountain chain that ran along the Hinterland, fencing it in – but from what? What lay on the other side of the mountains? She hadn't given that much thought either, but now that she was in the foothills of those mountains, she was beginning to wonder.

Suddenly, Vancy felt very foolish. What was she doing out here? She could be back in her cosy bed, not worrying about anything. If she went back now, she might not have been missed yet. Things could go on as normal – looking after the ponies, helping out in the fields.

True, she'd be back to being her usual self, feeling different from the others. It was as if they silently suspected her of something, or maybe even secretly hated her. And it wasn't as if she had *done* anything. Once again, the unfairness of it washed over her. They pretended to treat her like the other kids, but deep down they knew she was different. They whispered that old story about her – the one about the silver dog. And there was no party for her either. That just showed what they really thought. If they'd *really* thought of her as one of them, she would get a party, too. But it wasn't even about the party – Vancy didn't care about parties. No, it was being made to feel different. That was what she hated.

Erik and Lisbet hadn't helped either. Even though they'd always been kind, they still held themselves back from her. They didn't cuddle her the way she'd seen the other parents do with their kids. They didn't make stupid jokes or fool around. Of course, they were older than most of the other parents, but it made Vancy feel as if there was something wrong with her.

She rolled over on to her side and curled into a ball.

A vision of her real parents swam into her mind. They would be tall and proud – respected people. Her father would be strong and serious. Her mother would have long, shiny hair, the kind Vancy had always secretly wanted, instead of her own tangled mess. They would be so happy when they saw her. They would sweep her up in their arms. They must have been wondering, all these years, where their baby daughter had gone. They must have missed her terribly. The silver dog was responsible for that – it had obviously stolen her away. If there was such a thing as a silver dog, which Vancy very much doubted.

She sighed, burying her face into her coat. If she could only find her parents, then everything would be all right. She wouldn't feel like an outsider any more. She wouldn't …

Her thoughts were broken by a high-pitched ratcheting sound: *ee-ee-ee-ree-ree-ree*.

So there *was* something else out here apart from her. She held her breath, waiting to hear more, but there was nothing. She gripped the handle of her knife and curled herself up tighter, as small as possible. It was the darkness getting to her, she decided. It'd be better in the morning, when she'd be able to see things.

Another part of her brain answered: *Yeah, see the hyenas coming*.

Shut up, she told herself sternly. *You're out here now. You can't let your imagination run away with you.* Vancy sighed. Again she wished for her safe, warm bed back at Bassorah, and wondered whether she'd been missed yet. Probably not. Not till morning. And then she must have fallen asleep.

She didn't know how long she slept but, when she opened her eyes, it was bright, clear daylight. She sat up, feeling thirsty. In the distance, the sky was coloured with a faint haze of purple, like a drop of indigo in water.

Her first day out in the Hinterland.

Vancy jumped up, looking around eagerly, the worries of the night forgotten. She was one day closer to finding her real parents.

IV

No thunder tonight, but the air was stifling. Kerei turned restlessly in his bed, unable to sleep. It was late. His parents had gone to bed hours ago – or at least it seemed like hours ago. He swung his legs over the side of the bed and felt the cool stone floor beneath his feet. He'd get a drink of water – and maybe a little snack – then he'd be able to sleep, for sure.

Kerei padded through the sleeping house. Gentle snores came from his parents' room. Moonlight shone in through the blinds, making lines on the floor and across the table. He pulled open one of the drawers, looking for the box of almond patties, but they were gone. His father must've finished them off. He turned to the safe, which still contained a few interesting items.

Leftover vegetable stew? Hmm, nope. Spiced flat bread. Loads of fruit. Kerei selected a large peach and bit into it. Juice ran down his chin and he wiped it away with his sleeve as he took another bite. Then he poured some water from the jug into a cup and drank it down.

That felt better.

He was heading back towards his bedroom when something caught his attention – a rusty creak from outside. He would have thought no more of it, except that the sound came again. That was a bit odd. A bird-like screech, but no bird in Bassorah made a noise like that. What *was* it?

Curious, Kerei peeped out the narrow window opening beside the door. The night breeze felt pleasantly cool. Maybe he had just imagined the noise. But then the sound came again. A feeling of dread crept over him.

Kerei craned his neck and looked up the street.

Several doors up, and across the street from his house, Kerei saw movement. Maybe one of the ponies had got out. He hoped not, because he'd have to go and catch the darned thing. Then it would probably bite him, or stamp its sharp little hoof on his foot. No way. He wasn't going out in the middle of the night after a mad pony.

The sound came again – like fingernails scraped across a blackboard. And there was another sound now, a more familiar one: hurried footsteps, coming from the other, lower end of the street, down by the Keep. What was going on?

Kerei strained his eyes. There was definitely something moving out there. He could see a dark shape now. But it wasn't a pony, he thought. Certainly not a pony. As he tried to see what was in the shadows, the footsteps grew louder, more urgent, and he looked back to see two figures hurrying up from the lower end of the street.

When he glanced back the other way, the thing in the shadows moved partly into the moonlight.

Kerei shuddered. He didn't think then, but moved purely on instinct. *Got to wake my parents.* He ran – through the main room, down the dark hallway and burst into his parents' room. His father was snoring into his pillow. His mother, lying on her back, hands linked over her chest, seemed to be awake already. She turned her head to look at Kerei.

"What?" she asked softly, alert and frowning.

"You've got to …" gasped Kerei. What had he seen? It was something horrible, a bad dream, something like a … And those men coming up the street?

"Got to come," he hissed. "There's something outside!"

In a flash, his father was awake and both his parents were out of bed. As Kerei ran back out of the room, he heard the clink of his mother's arrow pouch being hefted. By now, other noises could be heard from outside – shouting, running footsteps. The bell on the Keep had started ringing. Intruders.

Kerei was at the window again. How did they get inside the Pass? The Pass was always guarded. He leapt back as his mother sprinted out the door – already in her long leather jerkin – followed by his father, close behind. At the door, his father paused for a moment and turned back with a worried look. "Stay inside, son," he said, and then he was off down the street.

Kerei stood helplessly on the doorstep,

watching as other dark figures tumbled out of doorways. An intruder! But what about the thing he had seen? Where was that now? And *what* was it? He didn't have a name for such a nightmare. All he'd seen – again he shuddered – was a gleaming eye and the flicker of a tongue.

He shivered and went to close the door. Oh yes, he would definitely stay inside the house. He'd probably lock himself in his room, which didn't have any window openings. He didn't mind being called a coward. Not after what he'd seen.

Just as Kerei was about to close the door, Squirt ran past. He spotted Kerei and doubled back. "Did you hear the bell?" he said in a rush, his eyes sparkling with excitement. "There's been an intruder. Somebody's got in through the Pass."

Kerei opened his mouth to say, *Yeah and I saw the thing*, but Squirt didn't give him a chance.

"Come on! Let's go down there and see what's happening." Trust Squirt to want to head directly into trouble. "I can hear fighting," he continued, turning towards the Keep.

Kerei could hear it now, too.

Spit shone on Squirt's lips. "Come *on*, Kerei. We can help."

Kerei noticed then that Squirt was holding a small, ancient-looking sword.

"Grab your sword or something and come *on*!"

Kerei coughed nervously. "I don't have anything like that."

Ignoring him, Squirt grabbed his arm and began dragging him down the street. The cobbles bit into Kerei's feet.

"I need some shoes," he protested.

Squirt wasn't listening. "Look," he breathed, "there's fighting in the Pass."

The boys pulled to a stop. There were Bassorah people with swords at the entrance to the Pass. Whoever – or whatever – they were fighting was invisible from this angle. Kerei thought of the *thing* he'd seen and felt his mouth go dry. He didn't want to go any further. He wanted to go back to the house.

But Squirt was itching to join the fighting. "Come on!" he urged.

Kerei watched as Squirt ran down towards the Pass. A man came out of the Keep at that moment, saw Squirt and roughly turned him around and pushed him back up the street. "Get out of here," yelled the man. "This is no place for you."

Squirt stood for a moment, his sword hanging limp at his side. Kerei felt embarrassed for his friend. Then again, Squirt shouldn't have run down like that, when the others were obviously dealing with it – whatever it was. They might have reached the age of maturity, but that didn't mean they could fight like the Patrols, or the men from the Keep.

Scowling, Squirt trudged back to Kerei.

"Typical," he spat. "You see?" His eyes were angry in the flickering light, but Kerei could also see that he was hurt. "They don't let us do anything."

Kerei fell into step beside his friend. "We'll hear all about it later," he said.

"Yeah, later." Squirt turned his head and spat on to the cobbles.

"Look," said Kerei. "Let's get up on Clay's roof. We'll be out of the way, but we'll still be able to see everything."

He and Squirt had been climbing on to that

roof for years – ever since they had figured out they could climb up the back wall using the rough stones as a ladder. And old Clay never knew any better. The old man was half deaf; he wouldn't even hear a mob of ponies on his roof. And the roof had a view directly down into the Pass.

Squirt's face brightened. "Good idea!"

Clay's house was just up ahead. The old man was standing out front, peering down the street. All the better, thought Kerei. They could slip around the back while he was distracted by the ruckus.

However, a few houses further up, a door opened. Vancy's house. Somebody peered out. It was Lisbet. She took a step out into the street and stood there in her pale nightgown. Seeing the boys, she lifted a hand. "What's happening?" she called.

Reluctantly, Kerei and Squirt carried on up the hill. They'd have to talk to her before they could do anything else. "Intruders," Squirt told Lisbet. "In the Pass!"

"Oh my, really?" She bowed her head as she digested this worrying news.

"Is Vancy around?" asked Kerei, suddenly

remembering that he hadn't seen the girl all day.

Lisbet raised her eyes and stared vacantly at the boys. "Vancy …"

"Yes?" said Kerei impatiently, wanting to get away.

"Vancy," she said feebly, "has gone …"

Lisbet led the boys inside and showed them the bed with its body of pillows. Erik joined them, and they all stood looking at the bed. Kerei felt funny about being in Vancy's room. He'd been in the house once or twice before, but never in here. There wasn't anything special about the room. It was pretty much like his own – except tidier – but it made him uncomfortable anyway. It was like hearing a secret. You wanted to hear it, but at the same time you didn't.

"I didn't miss her until this afternoon," said Lisbet, wringing her hands. "I hadn't been feeling very well in the morning and Vancy always goes down early to the Mill, so I didn't look in her room. Then I slept for a few hours." Squirt was shuffling from foot to foot now, obviously itching to get away. "She must have gone off last night," finished Lisbet.

Kerei hoped she wouldn't start crying. She

sounded as if she might.

Erik spoke up then. "Do either of you boys know where Vancy might have gone?"

"Nope," said Squirt, then added, "No, sorry."

"Kerei?"

Kerei was thinking back to that morning. "She wasn't at the Mill," he told the old couple. "I didn't think too much of it, though. I fed the ponies myself."

"All right," said Erik, turning away.

Lisbet was still staring at the bed. Tears were glistening in her eyes now. "There is no note," she said quietly, "but she has gone." Her sad brown eyes turned to Kerei. "Where would she have gone?"

Kerei shrugged. He couldn't even begin to think where she might've run off to, let alone *why*. Squirt was twitching at his side. This was getting embarrassing. "Um, maybe she'll turn up again soon," said Kerei, feeling stupid. If only his mother were here, she'd know the right thing to say.

But Lisbet nodded anyway and turned from the room. "I hope you're right," she sighed.

Kerei breathed his own sigh of relief. They

were being let off the hook. They could get up on Clay's roof now.

Out in the main room, which was smaller than the one at Kerei's house, but again much tidier, Erik was staring out the front door. He looked at his wife and put an arm around her shoulders. "There's nothing we can do right now," he said. "There is fighting down there." They all looked in the direction of the Pass.

"Yes," said Lisbet, "we'll have to wait until it's over. Then we can tell the Patrol. Perhaps they'll send someone out," she said, as if she didn't quite believe it.

"You mean, out into the *Hinterland*?" said Squirt, his face glowing in the lantern light.

"Yes," said Erik grimly. "Where else would she have gone?"

The boys stood in the middle of the street. A man ran past them, going up the hill. His face was smeared with ash. "They've set fire to the Lower Stores," he gasped, racing past them.

"He's going to get the water pipe," said Squirt dreamily.

"Yes," agreed Kerei. "They'll need the water."

"We could help with that," added Squirt, still staring down at the Pass.

Then they looked at each other. The two boys had grown up together and knew each other so well that sometimes they seemed to read each other's minds.

"We *could* help with that," said Kerei, looking back up the street, the way the running man had gone. There were other kids up there now, all ages. If Vancy had been around, she would have been one of the first to help set up the water pipe down the street. "There's bound to be something useful we can do, even if we're not allowed near the Pass," he said thoughtfully.

Squirt's eyes followed Kerei's. It was busy up there. It seemed the whole town was awake and helping. "But then," he said, as thoughtfully as Kerei, "we might just get in the way."

"True," sniffed Kerei.

Suddenly, Squirt grabbed his friend's arm. He'd had a brilliant new idea. "D'you know how we could really make ourselves useful?"

Kerei already knew what Squirt was talking about. He gave a little huff and looked down at his bare feet. He had scuffed the big toe and it was bleeding a little, but that didn't matter. What Squirt had in mind was bigger than a scuffed toe. He looked down at the Pass. "I don't know," he muttered.

"Oh, come on," cried Squirt. "It would be an adventure."

"Ye-es," said Kerei with a small shiver. "A *dangerous* adventure."

"As dangerous as staying here?" asked Squirt in a cunning voice.

Kerei remembered the scary-eyed thing he'd seen. Was that what was in the Pass now? Or was it lurking behind one of the houses? He glanced around quickly, as if the thing might be right behind them.

"And we'd be doing a good deed," added Squirt.

"Yes, but going into the Hinterland?" Kerei protested. "She might not even have gone there, anyway. She's probably hiding in the corn, sulking about something."

"I reckon she's out there. Where else is there to go?"

Kerei looked at his friend. "You just want to

go out there yourself."

"Well, yes," said Squirt, "I do." He had that cunning look again. "And I bet you want to, too."

That made Kerei pause. Did he really want to explore the Hinterland? The place they were forbidden to go? The place they were too young to go. The place his mother went, with the endless Patrols. She didn't even talk about what they saw out there. There could be anything.

But Squirt was right: they weren't allowed to do anything interesting. And suddenly, despite all his fears, Kerei realised that, deep down, he *did* want to see what was out there.

"Besides," said Squirt, "if we rescue Van, she'll never live it down."

Kerei chuckled. "True." The thought of Vancy having to say thank you was pretty good. That would teach her a lesson. All those times with the ponies when she had laughed at him. The shoe would be on the other foot this time. "All right," he said bravely, "let's do it."

V

The further Vancy went into the Hinterland, the colder it got. As the day inched towards noon, the sky changed from white to grey. The mountains to her left were speckled with snow. The girl put on her jacket, shivering. How could anything live out here? She stopped several times to drink a mouthful of water. She could tell by jiggling the skin that already there wasn't much left.

Still there was no sign of any kind of dwellings or town.

Footsore and weary, Vancy wondered how long she could keep going. A sharp rock bit into her foot, then she tripped over a scrawny clump of grass and fell on to the cold gravel. Something skittered away from the clump, running over her foot. She yelped. It was a dirt-yellow lizard.

Sheesh.

Stopping to catch her breath, Vancy glanced around. Everywhere looked the same now. Only the black and white mountains on her right gave her any sense of direction. She'd had no idea how big this place was. She had expected it to be more like Bassorah – easy enough to walk around in a day. But this was … well, huge. There was really no going back now.

She turned once more towards the horizon. Something flashed in the distance. A roof? A dwelling? Vancy shielded her eyes, peering into the distance. Something seemed to be moving out there. She could see two black dots now. Was it something good or something bad? Maybe she should hide. No, she'd try and see, first, what it was up ahead. Then she could think about hiding. Not that there was anywhere much to hide. But she could nestle down into a hollow or try to make herself small behind a mound of grass.

A faint sound reached her ears. A rhythm. It sounded familiar. And, again, something flashed. Vancy frowned. Good or bad? Hard to say.

It was then that she realised what she was seeing: two men riding on what looked like very large ponies. Were these the "horses" people in Bassorah spoke about? They were said to be similar to ponies, but taller, heavier, and with short hair.

Herit's Fortress was the only place that had horses.

Vancy looked around quickly for somewhere to hide. There was a rock, perhaps large enough to hide a girl. She got down behind it, holding on to her knees. She could feel the rhythm of the horses now, coming up through the ground. She could hear the rattle and clunk of the riders.

Putting her head down, Vancy prayed they wouldn't see her. The riders were getting closer and closer. Then, suddenly, they were all around her. She looked up, terrified. The men on the horses were dark and fierce, wearing black helmets and soft laced-up boots. It was the silver buckles of their harnesses that she had seen catching the light. Vancy could only stare in wonder. She'd never seen anything like it. And the horses – real horses! So big! Three times bigger than the ponies back in Bassorah. It was the horses that had found her.

She stood up gingerly and stayed absolutely still. The men hadn't noticed her yet; they were trying to control their spooked horses. The great beasts were stamping around the rock, eyes rolling down at Vancy. Dust flew into the air. One of the horses had foam on its muzzle. The other stopped stamping and moved in closer. It touched her shoulder with its muzzle, panting hotly on to her skin.

"Hey! It's a kid." One of the riders cursed out loud as his horse danced back from the rock, and then forward again. Vancy held her breath, terrified. She was going to be trampled underfoot by these huge creatures!

"Where have you come from?" shouted one of the men.

"Bassorah," said Vancy in a small voice.

"Well, I'll be …"

The men looked at each other. They shook their heads. Then one of them laughed. "This'll be a fine prize," he said.

The next thing she knew, Vancy was being lifted up and thrown across the front of one of the horses. In a flash, the two men wheeled their horses back the way they had come. Away they galloped, like the wind.

VI

Squirt was bouncing from foot to foot in his agitation. "How are we going to get it out of here without anybody seeing?" he asked.

Back at their houses, the boys had both hurriedly packed a bag each. Kerei had put on his boots and grabbed some food. Now here they were at the pony enclosure. Faint whinnying noises came from the stalls. Kerei wished Vancy was there to help. But of course, if she had been, they wouldn't be considering what to do next. Kerei glanced behind him into the street, where several people were running down the hill towards the Lower Stores, carrying the water pipe.

"Well," said Kerei, his eyes narrowing, "I have a cunning plan ..."

"Oh yes?"

"Yes. We make a diversion."

"What kind of diversion?"

Kerei frowned. Yes, what kind? He hadn't worked that one out. He'd have to think fast if they were to get away. It mightn't be long before things returned to normal. "I know! We'll get a pony as close as we can to the Pass, then you'll run out shouting about more intruders up by the lake."

"But …" Squirt was looking very doubtful.

"Trust me," Kerei hissed. "It'll work."

"Hurry up then and get the pony."

They peered into the enclosure. "Ah yes, the pony," echoed Kerei. *The evil ponies that would rather bite you than let you get near.* Kerei had seen how Vancy handled them, but he hadn't done it himself. Now he had to try and catch one.

Squirt elbowed his side.

"All right, all right," said Kerei. "I'm going."

He grabbed a rope and one of the halters off the fence and entered the enclosure. The ponies were coming out of their shelter. They would want Vancy, even Kerei knew that. She would soothe them, tell them there was nothing to fear.

Well, he could do that, too.

"Good ponies," he murmured. "It's me, the boy who gives you nice treats." A pony whinnied harshly. "Everything's all right, little ponies. Everything's fine. Nothing to worry about."

"Hurry up!" Squirt hissed from behind him.

Kerei cleared his throat. His hands were shaking, but they needed a pony to ride. Vancy had a head start. He had to get over his fear and do the job. He could do it. Just pretend you're Vancy, he told himself. Stride fearlessly up to one of the ponies and grab it.

The ponies were milling around in the dark, their eyes rolling. They looked really upset. Never mind. He was here to do a job. Taking a deep breath, Kerei marched straight in among them and threw the rope over a hairy neck.

"Gotcha," he breathed. "Good pony, good boy, steady now, steaaady …"

And then he was down on the ground. He quickly rolled over to one side, to avoid the trampling hooves. "Oh, bother!" He got up. "You little …" Now he was getting angry. He'd had enough of these sulky ponies.

Again he launched himself in. Heads butted

and hairy, smelly sides pushed against him. But he got his rope around one of the lunging necks, and this time, he quickly slipped on the halter. He'd got it on!

He started pulling. There was an outraged whinny, but the pony was coming with him. Squirt was at the gate, holding it open. "Come on," he said urgently, "let's get out of here."

Soon they were hurrying along the path behind the houses: two boys and a pony on a lead. Kerei couldn't believe it. He'd actually caught one of the smelly little beasts. He chuckled quietly to himself. Wait until he told Vancy!

"Shut up," snapped Squirt. "We're getting close to the Pass."

They paused and peered out from behind the stonemason's house. They could see dark figures in the Pass.

"They're driving the intruders out," whispered Squirt.

Kerei was again reminded of the strange creature he'd seen. The pony stamped behind them. Not a good sign. The teeth would probably come next.

"What d'we do now?" hissed Squirt.

"I dunno."

"What about your cunning plan?"

"It won't work from here."

As the boys watched, straining their ears, they realised the fighting was actually moving towards the other end of the Pass – out into the Hinterland itself. Kerei's mother would be out there, perhaps even his father. Squirt gave Kerei a stern look. "You know what we've gotta do, don't you?"

Kerei swallowed. Yes, he did. Forget the stupid diversion. They would have to follow the fighting into the Pass itself and hope to get away without being seen. He nodded.

"All right then," said Squirt. "On a count of three …"

Moving as stealthily as they could, the boys led the pony around the back of the Keep, making sure they stayed in the shadows. A dark figure hurried past, but the man didn't see them. Then they were in the Pass. A single lantern, high up on the rocky wall, cast long, fingery shadows in front of them. Despite his earlier bravery, Kerei shivered. They were really doing this stupid thing. He wanted to run back home and shut the door. He didn't want to go and rescue Vancy. She'd probably come home by herself anyway.

Up ahead, Squirt stopped and put a finger to his lips. Kerei also stopped. "Ow!" The pony bumped into the back of him.

"Look," whispered Squirt.

There was a knot of figures out in the open, fighting. Strange men in helmets. Herit's men? Was that what they looked like? Kerei was stunned by the sight of the strangers. So this was what his mother had to deal with out in the Hinterland.

And now he could see her. She was off to one side, winding up her hammer – a spiked ball on a chain, which she was revolving around her head, spinning it to pick up more speed. Then she brought it down. Somebody cried out in pain.

"Ouch," whispered Kerei. "That must've hurt." He felt a surge of pride for his mother.

But there was no time to enjoy the battle. Squirt was pulling him on. They hurried out of the Pass and veered hard to the left, away from the fighting.

With the pony trotting along behind, they hurried further and further away from Bassorah, expecting to hear a shout from behind at any moment. But there were no shouts, and soon the fighting was far behind them.

"Curse this pony," gasped Kerei, giving the animal another kick in the side. "Why won't it go? You would *think*," he said sarcastically, "that when it got the chance it would just take off, wouldn't you?"

Both boys, legs dangling nearly to the ground, were sitting on the hairy mill pony. The sun was about to come up, and all around them was an endless grey plain.

"It's just as well nobody can see us now," muttered Kerei.

Behind him on the pony, Squirt snuffled, but said nothing. It was cold, and they had no idea which direction to take.

"Oh yes, this is certainly one fine adventure," continued Kerei.

Last night it *had* seemed like an adventure. It was the first time either boy had been away from home. They had taken turns riding the pony late into the night and then made camp. Kerei had tied the pony's rope to a large rock. Then they had each eaten an almond patty before spending a restless few hours tossing and turning on the hard ground with the stars glittering above them.

Now, in the dull morning light, with a mist rising off the ground, things didn't seem quite so exciting. In fact, Kerei was about ready to go back home.

The pony leaned forward and delicately pulled up some dry grass.

"Of course," said Kerei, "we could just sit here and wait for somebody to come and rescue us." He gave the rope a jiggle, which the pony ignored. "Or until one of Herit's men comes along."

"Did I ever tell you," said Squirt's muffled voice from behind him, "you're a spineless weevil?"

"Yes, I believe you have," muttered Kerei. The pony lifted its head and sniffed the air.

"And that you know nothing about ponies?"

"I got us out here, didn't I?" retorted Kerei. He was still very pleased with himself for having caught the pony in the first place. Now, if only it would go!

"Maybe it doesn't like us on its back?"

"True," said Kerei thoughtfully. "They're not

used to being ridden. But do you really want to walk all the way?"

"Nope," admitted Squirt. "But maybe I've got a better idea."

He slid off the pony's back and wandered around, scanning the ground until he found what he was looking for – a bush with long, thick leaves. He cut a stem with his knife and climbed back on the pony behind his friend.

"You're not going to hit it with that puny thing, are you?"

"Have you got a better idea?"

Squirt brought the switch down hard on the pony's rump. It lifted its head, as if it had heard a distant call or whistle. Once again, Kerei thought that Vancy would have known just what to do right now.

"It's not going to work," sniffed Kerei. "That leaf is too soft. What we need is a really long, supple…"

But he didn't get to finish his sentence. With an angry whinny and a clatter of hooves, the pony suddenly took off.

VII

Vancy was dreaming. She was running. Running like the wind in a huge, barren place. Her paws were flying across the stony tundra. She was a dog – a big silver dog. She hadn't known she could run so fast. It was as if she could run forever, yet never grow tired. She opened her mouth, gulping in the night air. She laughed, and a bark came from her throat. The night rushed past, full of scents and smells. The night was good. The night was a shield. The single screech of a bird sounded in the distance and, without words, she understood the bird's cry.

Vancy woke with a start. Where was she?

It was morning. A haze of smoke hung heavy in the air. She sat up stiffly. The men on the horses last night … they had bundled her into a cage.

"Welcome to the Fortress," one of her captors had said with a chuckle.

Her side ached from lying on stone flags. True, she had a rough blanket and there was some straw – they had thought of that – but neither the straw nor the blanket made the stone feel any softer or warmer. It was so *cold*. Vancy thought about the cool mornings at home when she had snuggled deep beneath the covers of her bed, curled up like a cat. She stretched, pushing her feet against one side of the cage. Not a lot of room either. If only *this* was the dream!

But no such luck. Bending her knees, Vancy pushed her feet up against the ceiling bars of the cage, jiggling them to see if they were loose. They weren't. She rolled on to her side and gripped one of the cold metal bars.

Her dream reminded her of how she'd arrived at Bassorah as a baby. Left there, with a stone in her mouth, by a silver dog. Lisbet, superstitiously, had kept that little stone. Vancy used to take it out of its little box and play with it. Or rather, she had talked to it. She was embarrassed now to remember herself as a little girl, lonely for she knew not what, whispering her secrets to a brown pebble. Had there been anything special about that stone? Vancy didn't think so. It was just a funny little stone.

Where had that silver dog come from? And why had it taken her to Bassorah? When she was smaller, she used to nag people in the village about the silver dog. But people didn't like talking about it. Where there was one, there must be others, but nobody seemed to know anything about silver dogs. They were thought to live somewhere out in the Hinterland. They could have been just part of a story, except that several people had actually *seen* the dog at the edge of the fields that day. So it had to be real. The question was, what did the dog have to do with her real parents?

Vancy sat up again, careful not to bump her head. How strong was this cage? She felt around the corners of the bars, searching for weaknesses. There were joins at the top of each corner and bumps that felt like flat screws. The bars themselves were strong, certainly too strong to bend. What she had to do now was get out of this stupid little cage.

The cage was outside the Fortress proper,

against the main wall. There was a kind of large courtyard, enclosed as far as Vancy could see by a high stone wall. It was a bit like the courtyard at Erik and Lisbet's house, only much larger. From time to time, someone would walk across this paved area.

She could see the main gate, through which the men had ridden last night, in the wall to her far left. The entrance to the Fortress – a set of big heavy doors – was around the corner and out of her sight. Vancy had seen those doors the night before, when the men had brought her here.

Coughing, she stared out through the bars of the cage. A smell of burning filled the air. Dirty smoke rose up into the sky from a black chimney over to her right. There were snow-covered mountains rising high above the Fortress. The snow on the lower slopes was brown, polluted from the smoke.

Altogether, the Fortress seemed like a horrible place, but at least she had a little privacy. Maybe enough privacy to escape.

But what would she do if she did escape? There was nothing but rocks and clumps of grass surrounding the Fortress and no sign of other people nearby. Then there were the mountains, though there would be some cover in the foothills where she could hide. So, if she could just get out of this cage, that was the direction she would run.

Vancy got to work. They had taken her pack and her real knife, but she still had a small pocketknife, which she had slipped into her boot before she left Bassorah. Putting her hand through the bars at the top, Vancy worked the blade into one of the flat screws. It caught – only just – and she started to push, a little at a time, at the stiff screw.

She must have slept. The screw had proven harder to get out than Vancy had thought. Her hand had got so tired and cramped, she had had to stop. At some stage in the afternoon, a woman had brought her a cup of water and some bread.

"Please," said Vancy, "won't you let me out?"

The woman, who wore a scarf on her head, peered at Vancy. Her eyes were hard, nearly black, like some kind of animal.

"Let me out!" Vancy shouted.

The woman started back, surprised, then moved quickly away.

Vancy went back to working on the screw. Finally, she loosened it enough to wriggle it out. She hid the screw in the folds of her blanket and curled up to consider the other three screws that held the ceiling of bars in place. It was going to take her ages to get out. That was when she must have dozed off.

She woke up to find a face an inch away from the bars, staring at her. She screamed and sat up suddenly, bumping her head against the cage. It was a man – an older man, sitting cross-legged on the stone, chuckling to himself.

"Who are you?" demanded Vancy furiously. "Let me out this instant."

"Who would have thought …" the old man said softly.

A small lantern sat on the stone beside him, casting a golden glow. In this light, the man's eyes blazed yellow as a goat's. He ran a hand over his head. His greying hair was cropped short to the skull, which made his face look as if it were chipped from stone. He tilted his head to one side, considering her.

"And yet, here you are," he murmured.

Vancy stared back at him, a small fear growing inside her. This man wasn't like the men who had caught her in the Hinterland. There was something cold and different about this one. He looked like someone who would give orders, not receive them. Could this be Herit?

"Ah yes," he continued, as if hearing a good joke. "Here you have come, wandering back to me after all these years."

A chill went through Vancy. "What do you mean?" she asked, feeling as small and helpless as a child.

The old man laughed softly and held up a single finger. The nail was very long, thick and pearly. Van stared at it in fascination. "Let me tell you a story," he said. He shifted on the stone, making himself more comfortable, and began to speak in a slow, deep voice. "A baby was once born here and a prophecy was made about this baby. The prophecy told that one day, in the future, when the baby had grown into a young woman, she would destroy this fortress. So the baby was … disposed of – left out in the desert to die. At least, that was what they thought at the time, but later, much later, it seemed that she had lived."

The man leaned forward, close to the bars, and Vancy could smell wood smoke on him. She moved back as far as she could, shivering.

"And now," he said lazily, "I wonder how that came about?"

Finally, Vancy found her voice. "A silly old prophecy," she said, trying to sound braver than she really felt.

"Quite," said the man. "And yet, if a wise man didn't listen to prophecies, he would be foolish, don't you think?"

"It's got nothing to do with me," said Vancy. Although, in her heart, she knew that wasn't true. She thought again of the silver dog and the pebble found in her mouth.

"Hmm," said the man, glancing at his hands.

He seemed shy for a moment, but not for long. The light from the lantern flickered over his face. His yellow eyes burned into her. He waved his hand in the direction of the main entrance.

"Do you see all of this? I have a mighty fortress here. You haven't been inside, of course – and you never will – but my fortress extends deep down into the very rock itself. There are caves of precious metals, furnaces and many residents. I am the ruler here. I am the king of all I survey." He chuckled. "Do you really think I would let you go and risk all that I have built up?"

A wave of outrage swept over Vancy. "I can't believe this. I've got nothing to do with your stupid old prophecy. Let me go at once!"

The man simply chuckled and rose stiffly until he towered over the cage. He brushed down his long gown and picked up the lantern.

"Such a temper," he said with another mirthless chuckle. "Oh yes, quite a little firebrand. But not for long. Tomorrow, at dawn, you will once again be left in the desert."

Then he turned and strode away, leaving Vancy in miserable darkness.

VIII

The pony galloped madly across the desert as if chased by wolves. The boys hung on grimly, jolting up and down for what seemed like hours. Then the pony just stopped. Maybe it had had enough of two large boys on its back. Pulling to an abrupt halt, it lowered its head and bucked with its rear legs.

Kerei went sailing over the pony's head and landed in a patch of grass. Squirt went sideways in a clattering heap. The pony gave him a swift kick and took off.

Kerei hauled himself out of the grassy patch and watched the trail of dust as the pony galloped off towards the mountains.

Squirt was whining, holding his knee. "Look what it did to me. It's broken my knee."

Kerei went over and had a look. There was a bruised lump coming up, but he didn't think anything was broken. He slumped down beside his friend and stared glumly into the distance. All around them was desert. They could be days away from any other people – and from water. He dug around in his bag and found the packet of dried figs.

"Well," said Kerei, "we may as well turn back, I reckon."

"Turn back?" protested Squirt, disgusted.

"We can't go on without the pony."

"You can turn back if you like," said Squirt, holding his knee. "I'm going on."

"Even with a broken knee?" said Kerei with a smirk.

Squirt got carefully to his feet, checking his leg. Then he hefted his pack and set off in the direction they'd been heading.

"Hey," cried Kerei. Squirt ignored him. Kerei scrambled to his feet. "Hey, wait for me!"

It was dark now; the boys were tired and they had no pony. It seemed like the middle of the night, though really it was only two hours past sunset. They had walked for hours, until Kerei finally had to stop.

He dropped to the ground and drank some water from the skin. Squirt lay down next to him, putting an arm across his face. It looked as if he was going to sleep. Neither boy spoke; they were too exhausted. Kerei found some dried meat and passed a piece to Squirt, who only lifted his arm long enough to take it.

The night was getting cold and they would soon have to think about settling down somewhere. The next day didn't promise to be much better. Without the pony to ride, they might have to walk for days, or at least until their food and water ran out. And then what? It would be too far to go back. They would die out here.

Chewing miserably on his piece of meat, Kerei stared into the darkness. A bird called out a single sharp note. The stars shone brightly overhead. One star hung low in the sky. Kerei blinked. Then he rubbed his eyes, thinking the dark was playing tricks on him. Again he saw a very bright star close to the earth – but there was also a great wall of darkness rising up to meet it. There was something at the top of it; something that looked like a tower. Kerei squinted, his head tilted to one side, puzzling over this vision.

Then, suddenly, he realised it wasn't a star at all. It was a torch! A torch burning in the darkness. A torch burning on a huge building. He gave Squirt a shove. "Look at that," he breathed.

"What now?" complained Squirt, rolling on to his side.

"There's something over there."

Squirt sat up and stared into the darkness. Then he gave a low whoop and leapt to his feet. "We've made it," he said.

The closer the boys got to the Fortress, the larger it became. After their initial excitement, they had both grown quiet. Kerei was rapidly changing his mind about walking up to the Fortress and knocking on the front door. It brooded in the darkness, like a sleeping beast.

What kind of welcome would two boys from Bassorah get in that place? Kerei didn't want to know. But, if Vancy was in there … They would have to wait and see.

At last, they reached the base of the Fortress. A dark cliff of rock rose dizzyingly above them. There was no way they could get into the Fortress on this side.

"Crivets," murmured Squirt.

Kerei, craning his neck back to look at the wall, was thinking hard. "Did you ever believe those stories about Herit?"

"Not really," said Squirt. "Well, not since I was a little kid."

"Me neither," agreed Kerei quickly.

The stories were mainly about Herit attacking Bassorah. Stories about Herit's men setting trained wolves on to the Patrols. Personally, Kerei thought that was a bit far-fetched. It was hard enough training an ordinary dog, let alone a wolf. Yet, they all lived in fear that one day Herit would actually appear and attack them. That he would take their village – the fertile fields, the lake, the Mill – and call it his own. That was why Bassorah was always vigilant.

Then there was the thing that Kerei had seen outside Vancy's house. What if it was out here somewhere, waiting for them, ready to sniff them out?

Squirt was saying something.

"What?" muttered Kerei.

"I *said*, we should creep around this wall and see what's on the other side."

Squirt's eyes shone with excitement. Kerei envied his friend's bravery. Squirt was actually enjoying himself! This was just the kind of adventure he had probably been wanting. One day, Kerei thought, Squirt would be working at the Keep and going out with the Patrols, while he would still be working at the Mill, no doubt. For once, that option seemed pretty attractive.

"Okay," sighed Kerei. "We're here now. We may as well have a look."

Squirt set off to their left, with Kerei following behind. The boys kept close to the wall, in the shadows, and it wasn't long before the wall began to curve. Up ahead, the darkness was broken by a flickering golden light. Squirt stopped, holding out an arm to stop Kerei as well. They stood still, listening. Then Squirt crouched down, pressing himself against the wall. Kerei didn't need to be told to do the same thing. They had both heard the sound of hooves.

Suddenly, three men on horses appeared,

torch-light glinting and gleaming off their saddles. The men headed straight out into the Hinterland, cantering away into the night.

The boys waited until the riders had gone and set off again. Soon they could see where the men had come from – a broad stone entrance in the high wall. It was the main gate. A torch burned on each side. Beyond the gate rose the black tower of the Fortress.

Squirt gripped Kerei's arm. There was a sentry. They watched as the man walked around the wall, away from them. Kerei felt faint with fear. He desperately wanted to run away. "What do we do now?" he whispered.

Squirt nodded at the gate. "We go and have a look," he said, and before Kerei could stop him, his friend was darting forward. He had no choice but to follow.

They kept to the deep shadows on the right of the gate, hugging the stone. Then they were through. Squirt darted off to one side, flattening himself against the inside of the wall. Both boys crouched down low and inspected the scene before them.

There was a big paved area, bigger than any

open space they had at Bassorah. Luckily, there were no people around. Directly across from the gate was what looked to be the main entrance to the Fortress. Wide stone steps led up to a heavy wooden door. Everything was huge, impressive. They didn't need to see Herit to know that this was a serious place, a frightening place. What went on in that Fortress? Kerei shuddered to think.

He whispered into Squirt's ear. "Vancy's not going to be here. And, even if she is, we'll never get inside that place."

"We don't know that," Squirt whispered back. "Maybe she *is* here."

On the far side of the square, to the left of the main entrance, a figure rose up from the stone flags. Kerei clutched Squirt's arm. They both stared, goggle-eyed. It was a man in a long robe. Would he see them? Both boys crouched deeper into the shadows. As they watched, the man strode up the steps and into the Fortress, the heavy door clanging shut behind him. Kerei gave a sigh of relief.

Squirt nudged him and pointed. Where the man had come from, they could see a large square object. Was it a cage? The boys exchanged a look. They were both thinking the same thing. If that was a cage, could Vancy be inside it?

Once more, Squirt took off. Why did he keep doing that, thought Kerei. There was a difference between bravery and stupidity. His friend ran, bent over, right across the open gate and was soon crouched in the shadows on the other side, signalling for Kerei to follow him.

Kerei also ran, hunched over. Staying in the shadow of the wall, they ran along until they were opposite the square object. It was definitely a cage, and there was somebody inside it.

Squirt hesitated. "What if it's not Vancy?"

Kerei was wondering the same thing. What if it was somebody who might cry out? "We have to look," he said at last.

Squirt nodded. They both checked the square, but it was still empty, sucked clean of life. Then they ran across the open space towards the black wall of the Fortress, and straight to the cage. Inside it, a pale face with dark eyes stared back at them.

"What took you so long?" demanded Vancy.

IX

"So, where's the Patrol?" Vancy asked, peering up at Kerei as he struggled with the top corner screw. There was a lock on the door of the cage, but neither boy knew how to open the thing, so they had had to follow Vancy's idea about the screws. Using his own knife, Squirt was working on one of the bottom screws.

"Well … " Kerei coughed and fell silent.

Vancy glared at him. Of all the incompetent… It was just as well she was locked in the cage, otherwise she'd probably throttle him.

"It's like this … " Kerei began again nervously.

She continued glaring at the boy, even though she knew it made him jumpy. She could see right into his weaselly boy's heart, and she didn't like what she saw there.

"They were busy," said Squirt from his corner.

"Busy!" barked Vancy. She sat cross-legged on the blanket, looking from one boy to the other, trying very hard to be patient. They were, after all, rescuing her, so she should at least try to be grateful. "So busy they sent you two out instead?"

Again, it was Squirt who explained. "There were intruders. We sneaked out while they were busy fighting them."

Vancy hung her head. Intruders! A wave of guilt washed over her. She should've been there, helping. Instead, she had selfishly run off into the Hinterland. And now these two had turned up, which would make for even more trouble back home. It was probably her fault they were here at all. Kerei's mother would be furious.

"You should've told one of the Patrol," she said.

"What and missed out on saving your life?" That was Kerei.

"My life is perfectly fine, thanks very much."

"Yes, it looks like it," said Kerei, smirking at Squirt.

Vancy looked the other way, fuming.

Honestly, they'd *all* end up being left out in the desert at dawn. How could these two ever manage to get her out of the cage? And what had she found out? Zero. She sighed. Her parents obviously weren't here or Herit wouldn't have locked her in this stupid cage. Now where could she go? Even if the boys got her out, she had no water and no food, and no idea which direction to go in. But, if they stayed here, it would be much worse. At least they might have a chance of finding something else out there, apart from the Fortress.

Vancy's thoughts were suddenly broken by a hideous noise – a harsh grinding sound like rock being crushed. All three looked up. The square was still empty, but an ominous feeling now hung in the air.

"What was *that*?" whispered Kerei.

Vancy was barely breathing. Squirt, down in his corner, was frozen to the spot. And then the noise sounded again. It was certainly the cry of some kind of beast – but not a beast any of them knew. Vancy glanced up at Kerei. His face was white and his lips trembled. Squirt didn't look much better.

"I think," she said in a low voice, "that you should hurry up."

There was a sense of urgency now. Vancy started working on the last screw using her own knife. The boys bent over their own screws, working feverishly. None of them wanted to be around when that beast – whatever it was – turned up.

"Got it," whispered Squirt triumphantly. The screw rattled loudly as it fell on the stone flags.

Vancy expected to hear running feet at any moment, but the courtyard was silent. Squirt, who was in a better position than Vancy, took over the loosening of the last screw.

Meanwhile, Kerei had got his screw loose and slipped it into his pocket, taking care not to drop it. The wall of the cage was quite loose now. It didn't take Squirt long to loosen the last screw. Then the boys lifted the wall of bars away – fast.

Vancy popped out like a squirrel. It was time to get out of there. "Follow me," she muttered and ran across the square. The boys were only too happy to follow. Neither of them wanted to hang around in this place any longer. They could be discovered at any moment.

Vancy retraced the boys' steps back to the edge of the main gate and paused.

"Come on," hissed Kerei urgently. "Go!"

But Vancy put a finger to her lips. Outside, and around the edge of the stone wall, she could see what the boys couldn't – a sentry. She watched as the man paced up and down in front of the gate, a spear resting lightly on his shoulder. Beyond was the Hinterland – and freedom. But what to do now?

"It's guarded," she whispered. "We'll have to find another way out."

They ran back along the wall, keeping to the shadows. Vancy ran with her hand touching the wall beside her, feeling for a crack that might be a door or some kind of opening. But the wall was smooth, unbroken. What if the main gate was the only way in or out of the Fortress, like the Pass at Bassorah? But then, even Bassorah had a secret way out.

With a creak, the heavy doors of the Fortress started to open. They would be caught! What if it was Herit coming back to gloat over his prisoner? They would be trapped like mice in a bowl.

Squirt, who had got ahead of the others, suddenly stopped and signalled urgently. They quickly caught up with him. He had found a narrow set of steps cut into the stone, running up to the top of the wall.

Without a moment's hesitation, Vancy ran up the steps. She could hear the boys puffing behind her. Her own breathing sounded loud in the still night. Loud enough – she feared – to be heard by Herit himself.

At the top of the steps, a narrow alley ran off to Vancy's right – a lookout. Crouched over, she ran along it. It was like a tunnel, but open to the sky. There were arrow slits through which Vancy caught glimpses of the dim desert below. Then more stone steps appeared, going down this time. Vancy fled down them and around a corner. The lookout alley seemed to go on forever, curving ahead in the darkness.

"Van," a voice hissed behind her.

She looked back. Squirt was right behind her, breathing hard, but Kerei had stopped a short way behind them.

"What?"

Kerei pointed to the ground. "Look at this."

They ran back to Kerei. It was a wooden trapdoor. In her hurry, Vancy must have raced right over it. A metal ring was set into the wood and looked well used.

"What d'you think?" asked Kerei, his face pinched with fear.

Vancy didn't have time to feel sorry for him. She looked back over her shoulder at the long corridor of the lookout. Maybe it would just curl back on itself. Maybe there'd be another sentry at the other end of it. There was no time to find out. She crouched down and pulled up the ring. The trapdoor opened heavily and the trio found themselves looking down into a yawning black hole.

"There must be a way to get down," muttered Squirt, feeling around the inner wall of the hole. He looked up with a grin. "There's a ladder."

"Yes, but where does it *go*?" Kerei whispered anxiously.

Suddenly, the air was rent with a rusty screech. The hairs on Vancy's arms stood up. All three stood frozen. They could hear footsteps going rapidly across the square below. They hadn't been discovered yet, but it was only a matter of time.

Vancy looked down at the hole. Yes, anything could be waiting for them down there, but right now they didn't have much choice. She lowered herself into the hole, hanging on to the sides of the ladder. Carefully, she felt below for each rung and started to climb down. There was no way of telling how far down the ladder went.

Squirt followed next, then Kerei, who was softly whimpering.

"Kerei," hissed Squirt, "pull the trapdoor down after you."

"But …" Kerei's voice was high-pitched with fear.

But they'd be in complete darkness, thought Vancy – that was what Kerei was going to say. They would be climbing blind. Her mouth went dry. The three of them were clinging like bugs to the ladder.

"Kerei," said Vancy, looking up at the square of dim light, "you've got to do it. They'll see where we've gone otherwise. This way, it might give us some extra time …"

Above her, she could see the shadowy outline of Kerei, nodding reluctantly. He reached up for the trapdoor, pulled it down and they were plunged into complete blackness.

Climbing. Down, down. Feeling their way in the menacing darkness. Finally, Vancy's foot hit solid ground. Reaching out blindly with her hands, she found a wall. The boys climbed down beside her. They were crammed into a small space.

"Now what?" whispered Kerei.

"There's got to be a way out."

Vancy was already feeling around the wall with her hands. Stone under her fingertips. But then wood. "I've found something."

"Another trapdoor?" asked Squirt.

"A door, I think." She felt a metal ring. It turned easily and Vancy pushed against the wood. They stepped out into the grey foothills of the mountain.

X

"Rocks, rocks and more rocks," complained Kerei. "Whoever thought this Hinterland place was exciting?"

The three were trudging through the foothills of the mountain range, weaving their way between clumps of grass and snow, climbing steadily higher. Now they were crunching through patches of ice. Vancy was glad she'd thought to wrap the blanket from the cage around her before she left.

They had been walking all night, and now the sky was lightening. Silvery bands of cloud stretched across the sky, growing pinker by the minute.

They had decided to head west at first, away from the Fortress, rather than make directly towards Bassorah. It was Squirt who had thought that heading straight for Bassorah would be too obvious. "They'll be following us," he'd said.

So they walked on and on, waiting for the right moment to change direction. Perhaps they might even find a path higher up in the mountains that would take them back to Bassorah – a path hidden from the sight of the Fortress. As they walked, Kerei and Squirt told Vancy about their own journey, and how the mill pony had bucked them off.

Vancy couldn't help chuckling. "It's amazing you got as far as you did," she said. "They hate being ridden."

"Tell me about it," muttered Kerei.

"Though, right now, a pony would be pretty useful," added Vancy. "It's a long walk back."

"What I don't understand," said Squirt, "is that noise we heard back at the Fortress."

Vancy and Kerei exchanged a glance. Even though he had said nothing to Vancy about the thing he had heard and glimpsed back in Bassorah, she seemed to know what he was thinking. "I've seen it," she said in a low voice.

Squirt looked interested. "What is it?"

"They said Herit found it, inside the mountain,

a long time ago. It's his pet. He has trained it to do as he wants." She thought back to when the men had captured her in the Hinterland.

They had ridden through the night until, from her seat on the horse, she had seen a strange, loping creature catch up with the party. It had overtaken them, obviously knowing where it was going. The horses had whinnied in fear as it went past. Even the men had seemed afraid.

"They called it the Dread Lizard."

Kerei shivered. "I saw it, too – I think."

Squirt looked surprised. "Where?"

"Back at Bassorah," he said miserably.

They fell silent.

Thinking she had heard something, Vancy looked nervously behind her. Already they were some distance from the Fortress. There it was below them – torches still burning at the gates, a dark cloud hanging over it. In the pale dawn light, the Fortress looked like a grim and unfriendly place. She was very glad to have escaped. There were people moving about down there now. Perhaps they wouldn't be followed after all.

Sure-footed on the rocky terrain, Vancy

followed after the boys. She felt uneasy. But they had got away – hadn't they? She tried to ignore her feeling of anxiety and concentrate on the climbing. How long could they carry on like this? True, Kerei and Squirt had some food and water, but there wouldn't be enough for them to get all the way back to Bassorah. That was all Vancy could think about now – getting home. She had given up on finding her real parents. There were worse things, Vancy decided, than not knowing who your parents were.

She called out to the boys. "I think we should go higher now – try to find a path that leads back."

They started to climb up the sloping ground, picking their way through the rocks and snow. The higher they went, the colder it got, and the more the landscape changed. The rocks were getting much larger. Some of them were as big as houses. Others were sculpted by the wind into strange shapes. One or two even had shallow caves carved into them. There would be plenty of shelter, thought Vancy, if they needed to rest – or if they needed to hide.

Again, Vancy glanced back over her shoulder.

She didn't know what she expected to see, but she felt afraid. "Can't we go any faster?" she muttered.

Kerei rolled his eyes. He was panting from the effort. None of them was used to climbing mountains. Squirt, poised on the side of the slope, one hand on a large rock to steady himself, looked anxiously around at the others. "D'you hear that?" he whispered.

Vancy nodded. It was as if a dark fog was soaking into her. With icy fingers, it felt its way into her heart. Her breathing was harsh now, even though she wasn't climbing any more. Instinctively, she crouched down on the ground, hugging her knees.

"Get down," she hissed to the boys. They didn't need to be told twice. The three of them huddled into the shadow of a towering rock.

Some distance away, there was a scuttling fall of stones. They listened as rocky fragments skittered down the slope. The air smelt metallic, as if before lightning.

"Something's not right," whispered Kerei.

Then they could all hear it: a crunching of snow. The unmistakable thump of something moving over the ground. Down below, moving among the rocks, its head to the ground, was a large black shape.

"Crivets," breathed Kerei. It was his worst nightmare – again!

"It's so big," whispered Squirt.

The thing was hunting them. It would catch up with them soon. Vancy looked around desperately for somewhere to hide, but she could hardly move, let alone breathe. A heavy, suffocating blanket seemed to pin her to the spot. A blanket of dread.

But they had to move!

From the far distance came a shout and the sound of boots on gravel.

The thing was getting closer now. Picking its way through the rocks, it was following their trail. They could see its snout and open mouth, teeth glistening in the dim light. Its thick tail was swinging from side to side with each loping step. Scales gleamed dully on its back. Black eyes glowed, as if with concentrated hate.

The three stared as the Dread Lizard made its way towards them.

XI

Vancy glanced back over her shoulder and gasped.

"*What?*" hissed Kerei.

Behind them, standing beside the towering rock, was a large silver dog. It was nearly as tall as one of the mill ponies, its coat riffling in the breeze. Vancy could only stare in disbelief. The dog cocked one ear forward, listening. Then it motioned with its head, as if to say *follow me*, and disappeared around the rock.

Faced with a choice between the Dread Lizard and following a large wild dog, all three got to their feet immediately and followed the dog. It was trotting further up the slope and they hurried after it. In his haste, Squirt lost his footing and sent a few small stones rattling down the hill. They all looked back, expecting the Dread Lizard to be on them in a moment. It was still lower down the slope, but it had turned towards them now.

"Oh, crivets," breathed Kerei.

Up ahead, the silver dog darted behind a huge boulder. They found it standing beside a narrow fissure in the ground. Vancy heard a voice in her head, telling her quite clearly to get into the hole.

"Come on," she said to the boys, "we have to get in here."

"What if it's a trap?" hissed Squirt.

But Vancy was already climbing into the narrow hole, palms on each side of the fissure as she lowered herself down. She glanced up at the boys' frightened faces. "There are steps," she said briefly, then was gone from sight.

The raised voices of men sounded from below. The boys had no choice but to follow Vancy. One after the other, Kerei and Squirt also lowered themselves into the hole, though with more difficulty than Vancy. The gap was narrow. Vancy had made it look easy, but the boys were chunkier and had to squeeze themselves in. Kerei got a long scrape on his arm. Finally they, too, were inside, looking up at the light and wondering what would happen next.

The three were huddled against a rock on flat ground that felt dusty underfoot. The hole was like a small room under the earth. Daylight lit up the jagged edges of the fissure above, and they could see the shadow of the silver dog moving about near the entrance.

"What's it doing?" whispered Kerei.

"Don't know," mumbled Squirt.

There was a trickling sound. Vancy made a throttled noise in her throat.

"Well, I'll be …" breathed Kerei.

"It's urinating round the hole," whispered Squirt. "It's covering our scent."

Then, with a sudden rush of movement, the dog landed beside them in the hole. It made another *follow-me* flick of the head and started trotting ahead into the darkness. Quickly, the three prepared to scurry after it.

"Ow!" gasped Kerei. "My head!"

The roof of the tunnel was low – low enough for the dog to run with ease, but too low for humans to stand upright. Hunched over, they followed the dog as fast as they could. In the dim light, they could just see the shape of the dog up ahead and hear the click of its claws striking the hard ground. This underground place was not totally dark. Beams of dim light lit their way.

Now, from behind them, they could hear a horrible noise: a rasping, rattling sound, filled with hatred. Vancy imagined the Dread Lizard at the mouth of the hole. She prayed it wouldn't be able to follow them.

"Hurry," she whispered to the boys.

The tunnel twisted and turned. There were passages off to either side – black holes from which came currents of musty air, but they found the silver dog waiting patiently at each fork in their way. It didn't want them getting lost, that much was clear. Vancy noticed that the ground was gently sloping downwards now. There were also occasional patches of sudden and complete darkness, as if a candle had been pinched out. Again, they found the silver dog waiting for them, ready to lead them back into the dim grey light.

On and on they ran. It seemed like for hours.

Vancy pressed her hand into her side: she had a stitch, but there was no way she was going to stop running. Behind her, Kerei was breathing noisily, and up ahead was the hunched figure of Squirt. There must be tunnels running right through these mountains, like a honeycomb, she thought. It made her think of the Fortress and its vast underground rooms. Part of her would have liked to have seen those rooms. She wondered what they looked like.

"My neck hurts," Squirt complained.

They were in another dark patch now and had slowed to a walk. Vancy kept her fingertips against the left wall of the tunnel, feeling her way forward.

"Can't … run … any … more …" came the gasping voice behind her.

"Kerei, we're not running now, are we?" said Vancy through her teeth. She couldn't run much further either. It was a relief to be walking. Up ahead, she could see light. Not the dim grey light of the tunnels, but the warmer light of day – of outside.

"I think we're nearly there," Squirt panted over his shoulder.

They turned a corner and the light got brighter. The dog was no longer in sight. They seemed to be all alone.

"Where's the dog?" asked Vancy nervously. Had it abandoned them?

"It's …" began Squirt, but didn't finish the sentence.

The light was so bright now, they were all blinking. Then they found themselves at the mouth of a cave. Squirt was shading his eyes. He grinned at Vancy as she joined him. They could stand fully upright now. "It's out there," said Squirt, pointing, "waiting for us."

They stepped out on to a rocky ledge. The silver dog was lower down the slope, looking expectantly back up at them. *So there they are. Slow humans.* Vancy seemed to hear the words in her head, like an echo. Though it wasn't so much words as pictures. She had a picture of themselves as clumsy creatures, standing on their hind legs, and she giggled. It was a great feeling being out in the fresh air again; being in – she hoped – a safe place.

"Look at that," breathed Kerei.

A great plain stretched away to a hazy horizon. It was as vast as the Hinterland and just as never-ending, but different as well. There were trees – tall brown trees that dotted the plain, casting little puddles of shade – and there was long yellow grass, swaying gently in the breeze. It was like looking down at a huge pond of rippling golden water.

But there was no time to stand and look. The dog was trotting down the slope and they hurried after it, not wanting to be left behind.

The silver dog made its way along a path through the tall grass. It was a well-worn dirt track, regularly used, it seemed. The mountains were on their left now. They had crossed right over to the other side, thought Vancy with awe. This was another land altogether. Not the Hinterland, not anything she had heard of before. Even the Patrols hadn't talked about what was on the other side of the mountain range. And here they were! She felt like shouting with glee.

The path wove its way through the grass, past scattered trees and the occasional large rock. A flock of birds flew overhead in close formation. Vancy wondered where they were going. The dog, too, noticed the birds – glancing up at them for a moment – but its stride did not falter.

Finally, the dog slowed to a walk. It glanced

back at them, then turned to the left and headed back towards the mountains. There were huge boulders here, just like those on the other side. The dog finally stopped at a flat, sheltered place. Panting, the others caught up. Across the flat space was a large, dark opening in the rock: another cave. But that wasn't the most remarkable thing. Vancy sighed in disbelief and wonder. At the entrance to the cave stood a pack of silver dogs, staring back at them with shining grey eyes.

"I take it all back," Kerei said.

"What?" asked Vancy.

"You know, not believing the story about the silver dogs."

Vancy smiled. "Well, now you know."

She and Kerei were lying underneath a tree near the entrance to the cave. They'd had a long drink of water from a spring inside the cave and were feeling much better. The cave was huge inside – the size of a house – and in various corners there were litters of pups rolling about in the dust.

The silver dog had led them into the cave as if to show them around. They were followed by the pack of dogs. Wet snouts had nudged at their hands and snuffled at their legs. The pups had sat back in the shadows, watching them with bright eyes. "Did you hear that?" Squirt had asked.

Vancy had nodded, grinning. The cave was full of the murmur of dogs – except that it was all in their heads. Apart from the occasional yap or whine from a younger dog, the cave was mostly silent, but the sound in Vancy's head was of a busy, curious bunch of animals. Lots of images had also filtered into her mind – running through long grass, hunting, rabbits scurrying about in fear. And there was something else – something that seemed to be a man, but she had been too excited to fix on any one image. She held out her hand to a small dog and it gave her a lick. Moving her hand to its neck, she had run her fingers through its silvery hair. It was fine hair, yet strong.

Kerei had been surrounded by dogs, all sniffing and nudging him. "They're very friendly," he said. A pup latched its teeth on to the bottom of his trousers. "Hey, let go of that!" he cried, but when he tried to pull his leg away, the pup had pulled the other way. Finally, one of the older dogs had given the pup a nudge and it reluctantly let go.

"But why did that dog bring you to Bassorah all those years ago?" he asked Vancy now.

"I don't know," said Vancy, looking up at the feathery leaves waving above her. The sky was speckled with white clouds.

"D'you think it's the same one?"

"If it is, then it must be really old," she said.

"Well, I'm very glad that dog came along today when it did."

"Yes," said Vancy slowly. "It was as if it knew we were in trouble."

"And they can talk – sort of," said Kerei.

The girl grinned. "Yeah."

"Maybe one of them could come back with us and teach *our* dogs to talk."

"Then they could tell you what they want for dinner." Vancy laughed. But it reminded her of Bassorah and she soon grew thoughtful. "Won't your parents be worried?"

"And yours?" Kerei retorted.

Of course they would be worried. Vancy felt a pang of guilt at leaving no note, just a bed of pillows.

"But your mother," she persisted. "She's in the Patrol. She must be out looking for you."

Kerei frowned. "Yup," he said quietly. "But then, I left a note …"

"Really?" That made her feel bad all over again. "What did you say?"

The boy grinned. "That Squirt and I were going to rescue you and not to worry."

Vancy snorted. "Rescue?"

"And didn't we?"

"Well," she admitted, "maybe you helped. But I would've got out of that cage by myself!"

"Yes, it really looked that way."

She ignored his sarcasm. "But, note or no note, your mother is in the Patrol and she'll be looking for us," said Vancy.

Kerei hung his head. "Maybe. Chances are she's galloping around the Hinterland right now."

They were both quiet, thinking about that. Vancy hoped that the Patrol wouldn't go as far as the Fortress. She thought of the Dread Lizard, and what it might do if it were set loose. She shivered, then sat up. The grass was getting cold. "I want to ask the dogs about my parents. I don't know if I'll be able to do it, but I want to try somehow."

Kerei glanced at her. "How long d'you think dogs live for?"

Vancy bit her bottom lip, thinking. She knew what Kerei was saying: would any of these dogs have been around fourteen years ago? Would any of them remember? She felt a prickling in her eyes and blinked hard to force back the tears.

Kerei sensed her mood and sat up, too. "D'you think Squirt's all right?" he asked, changing the subject.

One of the dogs had brought them a dead rabbit, and Squirt had said he knew what to do with it. Vancy and Kerei had left him bent over a flat rock, skinning the thing. Squirt now had a fire going over by the cave entrance. Pieces of meat sizzled on a long stick above the flames.

"Ah, the original caveman." Kerei chuckled. He got up and went over to the fire.

Vancy stayed where she was, listening to their voices as they joshed about the rabbit. Once more, she saw her mother, her hair long and shiny. This time, there was a dark-haired man standing behind her, his hand on her shoulder. They were looking out at something, the way she, Kerei and Squirt had looked out over the new land today. There was a baby in her mother's lap – a baby Vancy knew was herself. As she looked, her mother popped a small stone into the baby's mouth.

XII

Gentle snuffling, soft sighs. The night spent in the cave with the dogs was like being part of a huge litter of pups. Kerei was curled up next to a silver dog. Squirt, asleep on his back, had a dog draped over his feet. Vancy opened her eyes at some stage during the night to find herself looking at a black button nose and a hairy snout. Grinning, she went back to sleep.

In the morning, they washed their faces at the spring, then ate some of Kerei's small store of figs and some of the cold rabbit meat. As good as it was, they would soon have to find some other kind of food.

Meanwhile, the dogs were outside, sunning themselves. Puppies rolled in the dust, play-fighting each other, nipping at tails and paws.

Several of the larger dogs had gone off into the long grass, their heads just visible above the stalks.

"Hunting," said Squirt, watching them go. Vancy could tell by the way he looked at them that Squirt loved the dogs.

Vancy sat off to one side on a rock, thinking. They couldn't stay here for too long. But what to do next? Somehow, they would have to find their way back to Bassorah. Maybe there was a way back from this side of the mountains … though it might be hard to find.

She hung her head. If the dogs knew nothing about her parents, then she would go home. There wasn't anything else to do. Besides, she already had parents – Lisbet and Erik. They had been her parents all these years. It was time to stop dreaming about people who probably didn't even exist any more. And, if they did, where exactly would they be living? In Herit's Fortress?

Vancy shivered even though the sun was warm. She looked up as the large silver dog – their guide – walked towards her. It seemed older than the others. The other dogs dipped their heads or rolled submissively on to their backs when it walked near them. It was obviously a male, the leader of the pack. The dog sat down next to her, gazing out across the grassy plain. Vancy wanted to touch his coat, but a feeling of respect held her back. This wasn't any ordinary dog that you could pat on the head or scratch behind the ears.

She followed the dog's gaze, but all she saw was grass and trees. What did he see? Though perhaps he wasn't looking, but scenting the air. There was a thoughtful look in his grey eyes. As if somebody was talking to her, a picture appeared in Vancy's mind. It was the man she had seen in her mind yesterday. The dark-haired man was standing by some kind of building, his hand resting on a fence. His head was cocked to one side, as if listening, or having a silent conversation.

Van looked at the dog. "Is that my father?" she asked quickly.

But the dog ignored her, as if she were one of the pups.

Vancy closed her eyes, trying to see the picture again, but this time all she saw was the

Hinterland. She was walking through the dry grass towards a large rock. On top of the rock was a bundle. Curious, she went to have a look. It was a human baby, vulnerable and weak, very young, wrapped in a cloth. The baby was whimpering, its mouth partly open. It was still early in the day, just past dawn, but she could tell that such a helpless creature wouldn't last long out here in the Hinterland. On the ground nearby, she saw a small pebble. She picked it up in her mouth, sucked it clean and popped it into the baby's mouth. The child stopped whimpering and sucked on the pebble. Good, thought Vancy, the baby will be quiet for a while now. Then she picked up the swaddled bundle with her teeth and trotted away.

Vancy opened her eyes and looked at the dog in wonder. "That was you?"

The dog's ears flicked forward, then relaxed back again. "But what about my parents?" she asked. She felt as if she was annoying the silver dog with her questions. She should be patient and wait, but she couldn't. "Did you know my parents?" she persisted.

The dog got up and walked away.

Kerei and Squirt were sitting under a tree. Vancy flopped down beside them. "I think there's somebody the dog wants us to meet," she said, feeling a bit silly. It was one thing being rescued by a dog, but talking to him as well! And it wasn't even "talking" either. It wasn't as if the dog had told her to go and meet the dark-haired man. No, far from it. He had put the idea into her head. Like planting a seed in the ground. She was certain the dog wanted her to go and meet this stranger.

Squirt, who was scratching at the ground with a stick, glanced up shyly. "The dog showed me that picture, too," he said.

Kerei cleared his throat. "Yup. Me, too."

"What d'you think it's all about?"

"I've got this theory …" blurted Kerei, but he stopped short when Squirt gave him a stern look.

It seemed to Vancy that the boys had already talked about this. "What?" she asked.

"It's just an idea." Kerei rubbed at an insect bite on his knee.

"Spit it out, Kerei."

"Well, I reckon the dog wants us to see this

man because he'll have some delicious food to give us. Something other than rabbit ..." He trailed off.

There was a moment's silence, then Vancy burst out laughing. Squirt followed.

"What?" protested Kerei.

"Don't you think about anything else except food?" said Squirt, wiping away tears of laughter.

"Laugh all you want," sulked Kerei, "but there's nothing wrong with a varied diet."

Squirt and Vancy laughed even harder.

The day was spent resting and dozing in the shade of the tree. They played with the pups and Vancy explored the foothills around the cave. The leader of the pack was gone for most of the day. Vancy saw him walk away into the grass, in the direction they had come from. She wondered if he was going back into the tunnel that led to the Hinterland.

That evening, one of the dogs dropped another rabbit carcass on the ground at Squirt's feet. Once more, they roasted it over a fire. Just as the sun was going down and the dogs were settling for the night, Vancy noticed the large dog returning through the grass. He hadn't come back with the hunting dogs and he wasn't carrying an offering for the pack.

"He hasn't been hunting," said Squirt, as if he'd been following Vancy's thoughts.

The dog walked over to where they sat under the tree and sat down with his paws stretched out in front of him. He glanced around, then looked at the ground.

Another image appeared in Vancy's head. It was the three of them, walking through long grass. Then there was another picture: the dark-haired man again, waiting. He's waiting for us, thought Vancy, as she turned to the boys. She could tell that they, too, were getting the same message. Then there was an even clearer image: it was dawn, and the boys were filling their water skins.

The silver dog sighed. He stood up, glanced at them briefly, as if to say goodnight, and walked towards the cave.

The sun had sunk below the horizon now, and the sky was streaked with mauve. Squirt lay back, linking his hands behind his head, and stared up at the branches of the tree. Kerei squinted into the distance. There was a quiet, reflective feeling between them, now that they knew what would happen next.

"I was hoping to stay here a while," said Squirt.

"Me, too," said Vancy. "I like the dogs."

Kerei made a huffing noise. "I hope that man has a horse or something we can borrow."

"Why?" said Vancy. "So you can eat it?"

Squirt snorted with laughter.

"No, stupid," said Kerei indignantly. "So we can ride back to Bassorah, of *course*."

"Yeah," said Vancy quietly. She was thinking about the mysterious dark-haired man and what he would mean to them. Why did the silver dog want them to meet him? Maybe it was something to do with getting back home. Even the dogs must see they couldn't stay here forever. They were humans and needed to be with other humans. Maybe it was something as simple as that.

"Either way," said Squirt, getting up to stretch, "we'll find out tomorrow."

That much was obvious: the dog had told them they would be leaving at dawn.

XIII

They walked and walked. With the silver dog in the lead, they followed the path through the tall grass. In places, the grass was as tall as Vancy's shoulder. Tiny flowers waved in the breeze. A shower of cold rain fell, then disappeared. The sky cleared. And still they walked, the foothills of the mountains always on their right.

Eventually, Vancy noticed a dark hole further up the rocky slope: the tunnel that led to the Hinterland. She shivered, thinking of the Dread Lizard and Herit. She was glad they weren't going that way. Instead, they kept walking.

The grasses sighed on either side of them and, as they walked, there were more trees. Bigger trees, in groups. Then the grass began to thin and the ground became rockier, the trees smaller and more stumpy. They had started to climb now. The path was steeper and it was getting colder. They were heading up towards the snowline.

Are we going into another land, Vancy wondered, and if so, what land? Could there be another land, apart from the land of the silver dogs and the Hinterland? It didn't seem possible. Yet, there was more out here than she could have imagined. One day, when she was older, she might come back and have a good look.

Still they climbed, higher and higher. Kerei was panting behind her.

The trees had now become thorny shrubs. There were more rocks, and beneath their feet was ice and gravel. Where are we going, Vancy wondered again. One part of her distrusted the dog, afraid that he might lead them back to Herit, but another part of her trusted him completely. Why would he betray them? He was their friend.

As the day started to fade, they came to a high, barren place. The trees were gone and there was a lot of snow underfoot. It was much colder up here and Vancy hugged the blanket around her shoulders. The grassy plain was far below them now. Where were they? Not in the Hinterland. Somewhere else. Up ahead, the sun was beginning to set – a red ball slipping below the horizon. Vancy's feet were sore and she was thirsty. She knew the boys felt the same, though they said nothing. Even Kerei was silent. They had all trusted themselves completely to the silver dog, for better or for worse.

Then, up ahead, Vancy saw something. It was a structure – a building – in a field of snow. The kind of thing a human would have made. Wooden beams and stone walls. A fence. The path led straight to it. As they drew closer, she could make out a figure. There was a man leaning against the fence, as if waiting for them – a dark-haired man. It was the same man the dog had shown her. He lifted his hand – a signal? A wave? As the sun sank below the horizon, the silver dog kept walking steadily onwards.

"Hail," the man cried, his arm raised.

He was talking to the dog. The other three were further behind. Perhaps he hadn't noticed them yet. But then his face changed. The man had seen them and he was staring at Vancy. There was a look of panic or fear on his face, as if he had seen a ghost.

"Dell?" he cried softly, craning forward.

The dog had reached him now. He stood by the man's side, looking back at Vancy and the boys as they made their way up the rocky path.

"Surely it can't be …" said the man. He looked as if he were going to cry.

Vancy stopped, nervous, and Kerei bumped into her. "Why's he staring at me?" she hissed.

"I don't know," said Kerei. "He looks a bit strange to me," he added beneath his breath. "Take care, Van."

Vancy glanced sideways at him. It was the first time Kerei had spoken to her like that –like a friend. But the sight of the stricken man was more riveting. He came forward, very slowly, as if walking on glass, until he was only a short distance away from Vancy.

"Dell?" he whispered. "Is that really you?" Up close, he looked haggard, his beard unshaven. His hair was jagged, as if cut with a blunt knife.

Vancy found her voice. "Do I know you?"

she asked tentatively, unsure how to carry on. A strange feeling raced through her. "Father?" she asked.

Suddenly, the man started laughing – a strange, high-pitched sound. Kerei jabbed Vancy in the ribs. "See, I told you so!"

Nevertheless, Vancy stepped forward to meet the man. Even though he wasn't the kind of father she had imagined for herself, there was still something familiar about him. "Father?" she asked again.

The silver dog had his head cocked to one side. He was sending her a picture, and it wasn't anything to do with her parents. She saw Herit, and a young woman in a brown dress. It made Vancy dizzy and confused. What was she supposed to think?

"Forgive me," cried the man, laughing that high, strange laugh again. "I'm not used to visitors!" And he turned on his heel and went back up the slope, ducking his head to enter the low doorway of the building.

At first, they didn't know what to do next, but the silver dog went to stand by the doorway, nodding at them to follow. They followed the man into a dim, wooden-beamed room with a fire burning in a corner.

"My sister," said the man, "was called Dell, and she looked exactly like you." He looked at his hands, work-worn and dirty. "That's why, when I saw you…" He trailed off.

They were sitting on low benches around the fire. The silver dog was sprawled on the ground, as if sleeping, yet the light glinted in his half-closed eyes.

"It was a shock," the man explained. "I'm sorry if I startled you." He hung his head. Words seemed hard for him. Squirt and Kerei exchanged a glance, wondering what they'd landed themselves in now. Firelight flickered over their faces.

"But I'm forgetting my manners!" exclaimed the strange man, leaping to his feet. He hurried across the room, leaving the others to wonder what was happening. There was a bench and a table in the corner of the room – a kind of kitchen – where the man started moving about.

"I reckon," whispered Kerei, "that, as soon as

we get the chance, we should take off – go back to the cave."

Squirt was frowning at the floor. Vancy sat silent, hands cupped between her knees, not sure what to think. Her father? Surely not. This didn't match the picture in her head at all. But who *was* this man? And why had the silver dog wanted them to meet him?

"Let's run now," whispered Kerei, his bottom lip trembling. "I don't like this."

But one look at the silver dog and Vancy knew there was nothing to be afraid of. The dog was calm and sleepy. Who knew, maybe this *was* her father. She was keen to hear his story – anything that might tell her the truth. "Let's wait," she said softly. "Then, if we want, we can run. We know the way."

Squirt nodded. "Yup," he said quietly. "Can't hurt. Besides," he added, with a sly glance at Kerei, "there might be food."

"Hmpf," said Kerei. "Food isn't everything."

Squirt snorted and Vancy chuckled quietly. For a moment, they could've been back at Bassorah, sitting around a campfire. The silver dog gave a sigh and made himself more comfortable on the stone floor. It was going to be a long night.

From the corner of the room came the smell of cooking. The man bustled around the table, setting out a large platter, then called them over. There were oat cakes, cheese, sliced fruit, boiled eggs. It was almost as if he had expected visitors. Yet he was apologetic.

"I'm sorry it's not more. It's all I've got at the moment," he said. "But, please, eat …"

Kerei helped himself and the others followed.

"I've got some chickens," the man explained, "and the goats give me milk to make the cheese." He rubbed his dry hands together. "The oats I grow myself …"

"The oat cakes are very good," said Kerei, his mouth full.

"Thank you." The man smiled broadly, pleased. He sat opposite Vancy. "My name's Tem, by the way." Vancy told him their names and that they came from Bassorah.

"Ah," he said wistfully. "I always meant to visit that place."

As she ate a piece of cheese, Vancy watched

the man's face carefully. He seemed full of sadness and shadows.

"My sister looked just like you," he said to Vancy at last.

Vancy looked at the table, blushing, and a silence fell. The boys helped themselves to more food from the platter, but it was as if there was just her and the man in the room. Even the dog seemed to be really asleep now. The fire crackled in the corner.

"We came to this land together, to Herit's Fortress." He stopped then, as if weary.

"I've seen the Fortress," said Vancy, wanting to encourage him.

"Yes … the mighty Fortress." He smiled, his lip twitching. "I lived in that place for many months."

Vancy finished her cheese and waited. Tem seemed to want to tell them his story. There was something about him she trusted. And she had a story to tell, too.

At last she filled the silence. "I was left in the desert, as a baby," Vancy told him. Kerei and Squirt were looking at her and she blushed again. She hadn't told them of her meeting with

Herit and what he had said about the baby and the prophecy.

The man's reaction was startling. He jerked forward, then made an effort to settle himself back in his seat again. "A baby," he muttered to himself, his eyes gleaming. "In the desert, yes, that must've been how it happened. I didn't think. Of course ..."

Vancy decided to push her luck. "A silver dog rescued me," she said boldly. In the corner, the dog's ears twitched. "It took me to Bassorah, where I have lived ever since." She was practically holding her breath. She thought she might explode.

The man looked up, his eyes dark with emotion. "I ... I ..." He didn't seem able to speak.

"My parents ..." began Vancy, then trailed off, not knowing what else to say.

The man looked at her. "Your parents ..." he echoed.

The boys had fallen asleep, curled up on the couches by the fire. It had been a long day, but Vancy was wide awake. The fire had burned down to embers now.

"Come with me," Tem whispered, not wanting to disturb the sleeping boys.

She followed him out of the room. They went through a doorway to a kind of veranda overlooking a yard. Snow glistened on the ground below. Vancy was glad of the extra blanket Tem had given her. It was cold!

Tem waved his arm at the night. "Tomorrow," he said, "you'll be able to see for miles."

Vancy felt weary. Her feet were sore, her head ached. Her breath came out in misty white puffs in the chilly air.

"D'you see that light glowing down there?" Tem asked.

Vancy nodded. "What is it?"

"It's the Fortress – one of Herit's furnaces that are always burning."

Vancy remembered the stink of smoke, the dirty snow. "Who are you?" she asked finally.

Tem took a deep breath. "If the dog is right," he began slowly, "and the dog is always right – and if your story is right ..." He paused, resting his elbows on a plank of wood, his eyes on the light below. "Then my sister, Dell, was your mother. And I am probably your uncle."

"On the other side of this plain," said Tem, "a long way from here, is a settlement."

It was late, around midnight, but Vancy was wide awake. She and her uncle, Tem – for she knew now that this must be her mother's brother – stood looking down at the distant Fortress. The torches on the gates were tiny orange dots in the night. Tem had showed her how to use his looking-scope, so that the gate leapt up to full size. She had seen a guard standing in its shadow.

"It's all mud houses back there," said Tem with a quiet laugh. "Very primitive. We were proud and pleased when the mighty Herit –from the land of metal and stone – showed an interest in us. He wanted a wife. Somebody to carry on his line. And my sister was chosen. It was considered a great honour," he explained. But he was frowning, as if the memory was painful. "If only we had known," he muttered. "If only we had been happy with our mud houses and our small industries."

Vancy heard a rattle of stones from below – it was the goats he kept underneath the house. She could smell straw.

"My sister and I travelled across the plain. It took us ten days of walking. When we arrived, Herit greeted us warmly. There were banquets and a beautiful wedding dress for my sister."

Vancy was trying hard to picture her mother as a young woman arriving at the Fortress. But another idea was getting in the way. "My mother married Herit?"

Her uncle nodded. "She wasn't beautiful, you know," he said, glancing at Vancy, "but she was special."

Vancy felt tears pricking her eyes. She nodded quietly. She knew how that felt. "What happened to her?"

The man cleared his throat, as if it was difficult to speak. "Well, at first all went well. We had the marriage ceremony, and Dell seemed happy, even though we were living practically underground by then. It was so different to our own home, where we'd mostly lived outside. But we got used to it. Herit even found a job for me." Tem chuckled bitterly. "He put me to work on building this place up here. It was supposed to be a lookout." He frowned into the darkness. "Anyway, my sister fell pregnant. And then ..."

"There was the prophecy?" guessed Vancy.

He looked at her, a look full of sadness. "Ah, so you know about that." There was a murmur of goats from below. "Yes, there was the prophecy. That the first-born – a female – would grow up to destroy Herit." Tem laughed, but there was no humour in his voice. "Such superstition! But he believed it. I was watchful as my sister came closer to having the baby. And afterwards. But it didn't look as if Herit was going to do anything. Then, one day, the baby was gone. Just like that. No explanation, nothing. I was looking after Dell by then ..." He trailed off.

"What happened to my mother?" Vancy made herself ask.

Her uncle wiped tears from his eyes. "She died from an infection, not long after the birth. There was nothing anybody could do." He rubbed his face with the sleeve of his jacket. "It was just as well, the way things turned out. At least she never had to miss her baby."

Vancy stared at the dark ground below their

feet, barely breathing. The truth seemed too enormous, too unexpected. She had always pictured … but never mind now what she'd pictured. That idea had been blown to bits.

"So, Herit is my father," Vancy said quietly.

"Yes," said Tem gently. "I'm sorry."

Vancy was curled up in a ball on the cot against the wall. It was the only bed in this place, but her uncle insisted she have it. He was lying on his back on the floor, beside the silver dog. It was a waste, really, because Vancy wasn't asleep. How could she be? Each time she closed her eyes, she saw Herit, crouched in the dark beside the cage. Herit – saying he was going to leave her out in the desert, for the second time. His own daughter!

He was a monster.

He was her father.

He was a monster.

XIV

The next morning dawned bright and clear. Vancy must have fallen asleep after all, because here she was, waking up. The others were already moving around and her uncle was putting bowls out on the table. She wanted to close her eyes and go back to sleep, then wake up in her own bed back at Bassorah. If only she hadn't been so reckless and run away. Finding her parents – what a joke that had turned out to be.

It was Squirt who noticed she was awake. "Hey, sleepyhead," he called. "Come and say goodbye to the dog. He's heading back to the cave."

Vancy sat up. "What, and leaving us here?"

Tem, over by the table, looked up. "You don't want to stay?" In the light of morning, he looked kind. Messy, too. He had some straw stuck in his hair.

Vancy blushed, feeling confused. "No, it's not that," she mumbled.

"Good," he said, brushing at his hair. Bits of straw fell out. "We've got lots to talk about."

"A war council," cried Kerei, over by the fire. He was eating something. It reminded Vancy that she was hungry.

Squirt and the silver dog were already at the door, so they all went outside to watch the dog pick his way down the slope, heading towards the grassy plain. At the bottom of the slope, he stopped and looked back. It was a single look, but Vancy saw in it a long story. Pictures flashed through her mind: of Herit, of the dogs, of running and the Dread Lizard.

Back inside, Tem brought a pot over to the table and ladled out steaming porridge. "I hope it'll be all right," he said apologetically. "My crop of oats wasn't so good this year."

It was delicious. There were plump raisins and sweet goats' cheese to sprinkle on top. For a while, everybody was too busy eating to say anything.

Finally, Tem pushed back his empty bowl and looked at them. "There are a few things I need to tell you," he said.

He started explaining how he had come to live up here after the death of his sister, breaking off all contact with the Fortress. Herit was preoccupied with the mining of precious metal and left him alone. "Perhaps they liked having me out of the way," he said. "I couldn't stay at the Fortress any longer and I couldn't face going home without Dell …" So he had stayed on at the lookout, and one year had quickly followed another.

Vancy looked up from her bowl. "But weren't you lonely up here, all by yourself?"

Tem shrugged. "Of course. But I also had the dogs. They'd come and visit. They're very good company, you know."

Then he told them about Herit's war against the silver dogs – how Herit had trained the Dread Lizard to hunt them. "Every now and then, Herit sends out a war party," he said darkly. "I don't know why, but he hates the dogs. He calls them vermin. Eventually, his plan is to build a second Fortress on this side of the mountains. If that happens, the dogs would be in real danger. There would be no stopping him then. He will own the plains and whatever else he can lay his hands on."

"He's been trying to get into Bassorah for years," Kerei muttered.

"For a long time," Tem continued, "I did nothing. It'll sound silly, but I was waiting for the prophecy to come true. You see, I kept hoping that Dell's baby was still alive. How, I don't know. Secretly, I hoped that somebody in the Fortress had spirited her away." He looked at his hands. "Then I started to plan my own revenge. Because of my sister and her baby. There's only one way to stop Herit – and I've been too afraid to do it … until now."

The boys exchanged excited looks.

Tem took a deep breath. "Without his weapons and metals, Herit will be powerless," he said. "I want to destroy the furnaces. It would take years for him to rebuild them. He'll be too busy to think about this side of the mountains."

Squirt leaned forward eagerly. "What's the plan?" he asked.

Tem looked embarrassed. "Well, I've been building up an area of snow, with a retaining wall," he said. "It's further along the ridge, in a line directly above the Fortress. There's the makings of an avalanche there now."

"An avalanche?" echoed Kerei. None of them knew much about snow, because Bassorah was so sheltered. It hardly ever snowed.

"Yes," said Tem. "A great wave of snow."

"But wouldn't it be dangerous?" asked Vancy, frowning. "What about all the people living down there?"

"They'll be all right. The Fortress itself is very strong. It's the furnaces I'm aiming for."

"Can we go and see it?" asked Squirt.

Vancy looked at him. Funny old Squirt. Out here, he was like a different boy altogether. She could imagine him in the Patrol, protecting Bassorah.

Tem folded his arms on the table. "So are you with me?"

"Yes!" said Squirt.

"Why not," said Kerei.

Vancy was silent. She could feel Tem's eyes on her. She was saved from having to say anything by a clattering noise from below.

"Oh no," cried Tem, getting up from the table.

"In all the excitement, I forgot about the goats." He hurried out of the room.

Vancy wrapped a blanket around her shoulders and went outside. Far below at the Fortress, tiny people were moving around. A plume of black smoke rose from the furnaces into the still sky. The white snow turned a dirty brown near the Fortress. It was hard to imagine an avalanche racing down that slope.

In the yard below, three goats came skittering into view and began nibbling at clumps of grass growing out of the snow. Tem appeared next, carrying a bundle of hay. The goats immediately trotted after him. He seemed like a kind person – more like the father Vancy would have liked. Yet here he was, plotting to send an avalanche down on to an unsuspecting community. Even if Herit was evil, she couldn't believe that everybody down there was, too. And Tem had been up here for so long, all by himself – what if he'd gone a bit strange?

Kerei appeared, also wrapped in a blanket.

"This snow is brilliant," he enthused. "Squirt and I are going to make a snowman. After Tem shows us his snow weapon."

Vancy turned her gaze back to the Fortress. She thought the avalanche idea was stupid and dangerous. There were more people moving around down there now. She squinted at the scene. It looked as if people were leaving the Fortress.

"What d'you think they're doing?" asked Kerei, shading his eyes.

"I don't know."

Then she heard him inhale. "Look at that," he gasped.

It was the unmistakable shape of the Dread Lizard. Vancy fetched Tem's looking-scope from the veranda. Through the eyepiece, the Dread Lizard sprang into furious detail. It was on a chain with a man following behind it. Its head swept from side to side as it loped forward. Vancy felt a chill run down her spine and lowered the scope.

"There are a lot of people out there now," said Kerei, his eyes fixed on the tiny figures below, now starting to fan out across the Hinterland. "It looks a bit like …"

"A search party," whispered Vancy, as if the Dread Lizard would be able to hear her.

"I'm going to get Tem," said Kerei. And he rushed away.

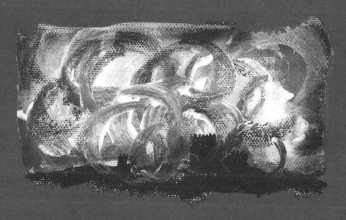

XV

They were all looking down at the Fortress. "I saw the same thing yesterday," muttered Tem. He was frowning. "I didn't know about you three then or I would've known what they were doing. Yesterday they were mostly searching further along in the foothills."

"That's where we met the silver dog," said Kerei. "He took us into a tunnel under the mountains."

"Ah," said Tem. "It all makes sense then." He looked thoughtful. "I wonder how long it'll be before they come up here."

"Why would they do that?" asked Squirt.

Tem shrugged. "Because they can."

"They might be here sooner rather than later," muttered Vancy, pointing.

Far below, the man was leading the Dread Lizard directly up the foothills behind the Fortress. They all stared.

"It's only a matter of time then," murmured Tem. "Perhaps as little as an hour."

As they watched, the man loosened the beast's chain and stood back. The Lizard started climbing the hill slowly, moving in short zigzags to either side, but always coming towards them. Vancy didn't need the looking-scope to know that it was searching for them.

"We must make haste now," said Tem. "Come with me."

They followed Tem along a rocky path leading to the highest point in the mountain. He was moving so quickly that the three had trouble keeping up with him. Up ahead, at the very edge of the mountain, was something that looked like a large log fence. Banked up behind the fence was a pile of snow.

Vancy peered over the rocky edge – the height was dizzying. Beside her, Kerei accidentally kicked a stone over the edge. They held their breath as it flew out into space.

"There's not much snow here," said Squirt doubtfully, from over by the fence.

Tem was inspecting the wall. "You don't need that much," he said.

"But won't the snow attack have to be huge?"

"It will be," said Tem, straightening up. "The avalanche gathers snow as it travels. See that field of snow down there." They looked down the steep slope at their feet. "My bunch of snow will pick up more snow as it goes down. It will gather speed as it goes. I've seen it before, up here in the bad winters."

"That lizard thing," said Kerei, his eyes fixed on the mountainside. "It's getting closer."

From below came a faint but unmistakable screech. The Dread Lizard was growing larger as it came closer. Already, it seemed to be a third of the way up the mountain.

"It must be moving very fast," murmured Vancy, with a shiver of fear.

"Oh yes," said Tem grimly. "Come on, you'll all have to help."

Quickly, they split into two groups. Tem and Vancy stood at one end of the fence, the boys at the other. Tem was digging in the snow.

"D'you see the rope?" he asked the boys.

Kerei nodded, his face pale.

"There is a rope attached to each of these wedges. When we pull them out, the supports holding the logs will fall down. The snow will do the rest. All right?"

Though he had just told them how it would work, Vancy found it all difficult to believe. She knew nothing about avalanches. How could this bit of snow even reach the foothills, let alone destroy the furnaces? But, with the Dread Lizard coming, what else could they do?

"On a count of three," cried Tem. "One …" Vancy gripped her end of the cold rope.

"Two …" Beside her, her uncle was holding the rope tight. He glanced at Vancy. "It's for the best," he said quickly. "You'll see." Then he started to haul on the rope. "Three!"

The boys had pulled out the wedge at their end and the two supports bumped free and flew over the edge. They all jumped back, getting out of the way as the wall of logs collapsed with a huge clatter that echoed against the rocks. The noise would have been heard for miles. Below,

Vancy saw the Dread Lizard look up.

The snow started to roll down the slope like a giant fist. It moved slowly forward at first, then, with a puff, it took off, crashing down the mountainside.

"Look at that," breathed an awestruck Kerei.

"It *is* getting bigger," cried Squirt.

The snow went faster and faster, as if it was running, growing as it went.

Suddenly, in a flurry, the snow hit the Dread Lizard. The beast flipped gracefully into the air, then bounced heavily on the rocky slope and back into the path of the rushing snow. Soon it, too, was careering down the slope – Lizard and avalanche, both crashing towards the Fortress.

From the plain, there came a tiny shout. People were looking up at the mountain.

"Get down," said Tem quickly. "They'll see us."

They lay down in the snow, oblivious to the cold that came seeping through their clothes, and watched as the avalanche hit the Fortress.

"Crivets," whispered Kerei.

Vancy could hardly believe her eyes. The snow had crashed on to the stone so hard it had broken a hole in the side of the Fortress. For a moment, all was still, except for the echo of the snow landing on the Fortress. Then, suddenly, there was a huge explosion. Vancy ducked her head as, far below, chunks of stone flew into the air.

"What was *that*?" cried Squirt.

Tem's eyes were huge. "Heat – cold – it's caused an explosion." There was a heavy rumbling, like thunder. Then another blast, from deeper down. "The caves," he murmured.

The people out on the plain were now running in all directions. They looked like panicking ants, but one dark figure was hurrying back towards the source of the explosion. Vancy lifted the looking-scope. *Herit*, she thought grimly, *my real father*. Seen through the scope, his face was pale with anger.

Another explosion rocked the mountain, more muted than the other two, obviously deeper in the ground. Tem was shaking his head. "Who would've thought," he muttered. "It's destroying the lower furnaces as well."

The dark figure of Herit lurched to a stop and, through the scope, Vancy saw him raise a fist to the mountains. It was as if he were cursing *her*. His lips were drawn back in a snarl. She quickly passed the scope to Tem.

"Ah," he said quietly. "He has guessed." He handed the scope back to Vancy.

"Will he be furious?" she asked.

"Oh yes," said Tem, "and he has a long memory. He will seek revenge. But, before that, he'll have to rebuild his precious Fortress, and that will take a long time. It won't stop him forever, but …"

Vancy shivered as they stared at the tumult below. She hoped it wouldn't mean more trouble for Bassorah. Or the silver dogs.

"It won't be safe for me to stay here any more," said Tem, getting stiffly to his feet as the others gathered around him.

"But where will you go?" asked Vancy.

He shrugged. "Perhaps back to my village. It's time I went back."

Vancy brushed the snow off her front. "Maybe first," she said shyly, "you could come back to Bassorah with us?"

Tem nodded. "Yes, I'd like that." He looked back down at the burning Fortress. "But come, we must go!"

They hurried back along the path to the house.

XVI

They packed as much as they could carry between them – food, dishes and bedding. The chickens went into a wicker basket, which Squirt picked up. Then Tem roped the three goats together and handed the rope to Kerei.

"Why do *I* always end up with the animals? I don't even *like* animals!"

Vancy giggled. "No, but they like you."

"Shut up," he muttered. "You, too," he said to Squirt.

"I haven't said anything," Squirt protested.

"No," sniffed Kerei, "but you were going to." One of the goats started nibbling at his jacket. He slapped it away. "And you – behave yourself!"

The goats stamped their hooves in the snow as they waited outside. Tem made one last tour of the house and shut the door firmly behind him. "It's been a good home to me, this place," he said. "I'll miss it." Then he looked down the slope at Vancy and the boys and grinned. "Let's get going."

Tem led them along the ridge, heading east, towards Bassorah. Below, to their right, was the vast Hinterland, spread out below them, grey in the fading light. They were following a track that Tem said would take them along the top of the mountain range. They'd spend the night in the mountains, then head down an old river bed. They could make their way down into the plains in the morning.

They walked silently in single file. None of them wanted to make too much noise. As Tem said, sound carried in the mountains.

An orange moon appeared, casting some light on the rocky path. Vancy found herself walking next to Tem, who was laden down with a huge pack.

"Do you think that was the end of the Dread Lizard?" she asked quietly.

"I hope so," said Tem, glancing at her.

"Will he come after us?" asked Vancy,

referring to Herit.

Tem shifted the load on his back. "Not immediately," he said. "But perhaps later. He will probably come looking for me first."

"But won't that put your home in danger?"

"I hope not," he said ruefully.

"You're sad to be going, aren't you?" said Vancy.

He nodded. "I've spent a big part of my life up in these mountains," he said.

"I feel like that about Bassorah," said Vancy. "Though I didn't know it would be like that until after I'd left."

"Sometimes," said Tem slowly, "you have to leave something behind to really start caring about it."

Vancy smiled. She was looking forward to going home – for Bassorah *was* her home. Even without a silly coming-of-age party. It might only have been a few days since she'd left, but everything had changed. The Vancy who had cried about not having her own party was gone now.

The next morning, after a fitful night trying to get some rest among the rocks, they climbed down out of the mountains.

Late that afternoon, Kerei stopped and squinted into the distance. "Isn't that …?"

Far ahead of them, they could see a group of people, also heading towards Bassorah.

"Hey!" shouted Kerei, racing forward, the goats running along behind him.

"Kerei, no!" cried Squirt, tearing after him. With his longer legs, Tem sprinted past Squirt and grabbed Kerei's shirt.

"They could be from Herit," he panted.

"No, no," cried Kerei, his eyes bright. "Look, they're from Bassorah – it's the Patrol."

"He's right," said Vancy, catching up with them. "That's one of the ponies with them."

The party had heard the noise behind them now and were starting back in their direction. The mill pony could be seen clearly – it *was* the Patrol. Kerei took off again, forgetting the goats completely, running towards a figure that came out from the group to meet him. Soon they were hugging tightly.

"His mother," explained Vancy.

"Ah," said Tem. "But what are they doing so far from home?"

"Looking for us, I should think," she said, blushing.

Kerei's mother, a tall, serious woman, was approaching them. "Hail," she called. "Where have you come from?" she demanded. "We've been searching the Hinterland for the last two days and there's been no sign of you. I've been worried sick. We were just heading back for fresh supplies."

Kerei was gabbling at her side. "You should've seen the Fortress, we were right inside it and –"

Her eyes widened with concern. "You were inside the Fortress?"

"And there were enormous dogs that could talk and … "

"Kerei," said his mother, holding up her hand, "slow down. You can tell me all about it on the way home. But who is this stranger?" she asked, turning to Tem.

Vancy quickly introduced her uncle. The rest of the story, she hoped, Tem could tell for himself. She didn't yet have the words for all of it. And what would people think when they found out that Herit was her father?

So Tem, Vancy and the boys resumed their trek back to Bassorah, now in the company of the Patrol. Kerei walked alongside his mother; he was nearly as tall as her now. Vancy led the goats. The mill pony nudged her side, kicking out jealously with its rear legs when the goats got too close. Happy to see it again, she stroked its shaggy mane.

Squirt caught up with her. "I'm going to be in trouble when we get back."

"Me, too," said Vancy ruefully. She blushed to think of the pillows she had stuffed into her bed. "We'll probably get the Four-day Punishment." It was the most serious punishment in Bassorah for a young person: four days spent cleaning the cobbles, with everybody looking at you.

"Still, it's only four days, right?" said Squirt with a grin.

"Right," said Vancy. There were worse things than cleaning cobbles.

Late the following day, they reached Bassorah.

Tem looked up at the Pass in wonder. "I had heard rumours about Bassorah," he said admiringly, "but I never imagined this ..."

"Wait till you see inside," said Squirt, racing ahead.

As they walked up the cobbled main street of Bassorah, people came out of their houses to greet them. Tears welled up in Vancy's eyes. Up ahead, an older couple waited, standing side by side, their arms around each other.

"Here, take these," she said to Tem, handing him the goats.

Vancy ran up the hill to Lisbet and Erik. The old couple held out their arms. Vancy was *home*.

XVII

Asleep in her bed, Vancy was dreaming of Herit. He was wandering alone in the Hinterland, dressed in a dark cloak. The stamping of his boots echoed loudly on the gravel. His yellow eyes were bloodshot and he looked as old as an ancient lizard. All around him was dust, stones and clumps of grass.

Herit kicked at a rock and sent it flying. He stared up at the heavy grey clouds and snarled. Then he raised his fist and shook it at the sky.